# FOUR SECONDS

# FOUR SECONDS

### All the Time You Need to
### Stop Counter-Productive Habits
### and Get the Results You Want

## PETER BREGMAN

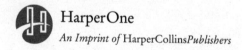

HarperOne
*An Imprint of* HarperCollins*Publishers*

HarperOne

FOUR SECONDS: *All the Time You Need to Stop Counter-Productive Habits and Get the Results You Want.* Copyright © 2015 by Peter Bregman. All rights reserved. Printed in the United States of America. No part of this book may be used or reproduced in any manner whatsoever without written permission except in the case of brief quotations embodied in critical articles and reviews. For information address HarperCollins Publishers, 195 Broadway, New York, NY 10007.

HarperCollins books may be purchased for educational, business, or sales promotional use. For information please e-mail the Special Markets Department at SPsales@harpercollins.com.

HarperCollins website: http://www.harpercollins.com

HarperCollins®, 📖®, and HarperOne™ are trademarks of Harper-Collins Publishers.

FIRST EDITION

*Designed by Janet M. Evans*

Library of Congress Cataloging-in-Publication Data is available upon request.

ISBN 978–0–06–237241–3

15 16 17 18 19 RRD(H) 10 9 8 7 6 5 4 3 2 1

*To Mama and Papa.*

*Thank you for loving me,*
*believing in me,*
*and supporting me.*
*I love you.*

# CONTENTS

# FOUR SECONDS

# INTRODUCTION

**I WAS WALKING DOWN FORTY-EIGHTH STREET IN MIDTOWN MANHATTAN,** when a man, well-dressed in a nice suit and shined shoes, with coiffed hair, and a leather briefcase, brushed by me. Then I saw him turn his head and spit out his gum.

I kept my eyes on the wad of gum to be sure I didn't step on it. The gum flew maybe three feet in front of me, bounced off a tree, and then rolled onto the sidewalk, landing right underneath his foot as he took his next step. He kept walking without noticing his own bright blue gum stuck to the sole of his shoe.

I laughed out loud.

And then I got to thinking. How often do we all do the same thing? How often do we take an action that we think is in our interest but ultimately ends up as gum stuck to our shoes? How often do we engage in behaviors that backfire?

Sometimes the ways in which our actions work against our interests are blatantly obvious—and easy to avoid. I just heard a story of someone who worked in a senior role at a Wall Street bank. Like the bank, he was highly leveraged; he'd bought an apartment well beyond his means. When he heard he wouldn't be getting a bonus as big as he'd expected, he yelled and cursed and disparaged his boss to other people in the firm. Now he doesn't have a bonus or a job.

Other times our self-sabotaging ways are more subtle, like the time I was running late for dinner with my wife, Eleanor. We had agreed to meet at a restaurant at seven o'clock, and it was already half past. I felt guilty but had been stuck in a client meeting that ran over. When I arrived, I apologized and told her I didn't mean to be late.

"You never *mean* to be late," she answered. Uh oh. She was mad.

"I'm sorry, sweetie," I said, "but it was unavoidable." I explained why I was late, describing details about the client meeting, maybe exaggerating a little to convey to her how important, how inescapable the meeting really was.

But instead of soothing her, I only made things worse. Now she was angry *and* annoyed.

Which made *me* angry and self-righteous. "Look," I said, "I'm working really hard."

The conversation continued to spiral down, each of us reacting to the other's response. We both wanted the same thing—to enjoy a nice dinner together. But our reflexive responses moved us apart, and we ended up feeling separate and angry, the exact opposite of what we intended.

The culprit: our counter-productive, knee-jerk reactions.

My knee-jerk reaction to being late was to offer an explanation. Eleanor's knee-jerk reaction to my explanation was impatience. My knee-jerk reaction to Eleanor's impatience was anger. And on and on the argument went, each of us mindlessly following our instinct-driven script, no matter how ineffective.

Obviously, I didn't *intend* to get into an argument with Eleanor. In fact, the reason I offered an explanation for my lateness was *not* to get into a fight. Yet, at the end of the day, my intention alone wasn't the most important thing. What mattered even more was how my action—explaining my lateness—affected Eleanor. Pretty poorly, it turned out. I basically spit out my gum and then stepped on it.

## When Bad Habits Happen to Good People

The basic things we all want—fulfilling relationships, accomplishments of which we're proud, meaningful success at work, to be of service to others, peace of mind—are surprisingly straightforward to achieve. But, in many cases, our best efforts to achieve them are built on habits and behaviors that, simply put, don't work.

When we feel overwhelmed and stressed by our growing to-do list, our knee-jerk reaction is to work longer hours and pack more into the hours we are already working. We multitask, dash from meeting to meeting, sneak e-mails under the conference-room table, and work early in the morning and late into the night. Our intention is to reduce our stress and overload. But our actions have the exact opposite effect: we end up more stressed and more overloaded.

Or we say things we think will impress someone but, instead, prompt rejection. We reach out to comfort a friend but, somehow, make her more upset. We give a team a pep talk, but without knowing why, we discourage them.

Each time we feel stunned. *What just happened?* we wonder. In the end, we spend days trying to repair the damage of those knee-jerk reactions that have backfired on us. We spend countless hours and energy thinking about what we said, talking to others about how we handled a situation, planning our next move, and maybe even walking the long way to the bathroom so we don't have to pass someone we've inadvertently offended in the hallway.

## Four Seconds to a Better Habit

There is good news: this is not a hard problem to solve. In fact, all you need is four seconds. Four seconds is the amount of time required to take a single breath. That short pause is all you need to see where you're going wrong and to make a little shift.

And I mean little. The alternatives I suggest in the pages that follow are amazingly straightforward. They give you the results you want, and you won't have to spin your wheels endlessly. They are ways of thinking, speaking, and acting—ways of being— that are simpler than the old ways and far more effective. They take less time and less energy. They help you become hyperproductive without being hyper.

In my book, *18 Minutes: Find Your Focus, Master Distraction, and Get the Right Things Done,* I offered a way for you to regain your focus and reshape your days around what matters most to you. I asked you to be strategic and intentional about *what* you do.

In *Four Seconds,* I'll show you how to be strategic and intentional—at the speed of light—about *how* you do what you do. *18 Minutes* helped you focus on the right things. *Four Seconds* will help you get the most out of that focus.

After all, it's not enough to excel at managing your time; you need to excel at using that time powerfully. *How* you act *during* those hours determines your success: how you frame your mind, how you relate to others, how you speak and act at work and with your teams. The goal is not just to survive a busy life but to thrive in your most important endeavors and relationships.

You'll learn to replace time-sucking, energy-wasting, counterproductive knee-jerk reactions with new habits and behaviors that are time saving, energy boosting, and productive. You'll learn new ways of living, working, and connecting in this fast-paced world that bring results *and* peace.

## A New Habit Is Born

What could I have done differently when I arrived late so my valuable time with Eleanor was spent enjoyably instead of fighting? I could have taken just four seconds—enough time for a deep breath, a pause, a reset of my perspective—and then resisted the urge to explain my lateness, and instead acknowledged Eleanor's experience of waiting for me:

"I'm sorry I'm late. You've been sitting here for thirty minutes, and that's frustrating. And I know it's not the first time. I can see how it seems like I think being with a client gives me permission to be late. That's disrespectful of your time, and I'm sorry you had to wait here for so long."

This is easier said than done. My intuitive, gut-instinct, knee-jerk reaction is to validate my tardiness rather than my wife's feelings. Doing so makes *me* feel better, like I'm not so bad for being late because there's a specific reason. But the intuitive response is counter-productive. While it makes me feel better, it makes Eleanor—who's been waiting for me—feel worse. It reinforces the point that whatever I was doing that made me late is clearly more important than she is. And just like that, without even realizing why, our nice evening is destroyed.

On the other hand, avoiding any explanation but reflecting on how my lateness affects Eleanor, while counterintuitive, actually makes her feel better. That's because it shows her that I see her. And it's an admission that there's no good explanation for keeping her waiting. And just like that, our nice evening is saved.

And a new habit is born. When I'm late, my new knee-jerk response is still to apologize, but now I don't explain—or make excuses for—why I'm late. Instead, I acknowledge the other person's experience of waiting for me.

There's an added bonus to this new habit: I'm late less often. Explaining to Eleanor how my lateness affected her made me want to change in general. I don't want to be disrespectful of her or anyone else's time. And I don't want her or others to feel frustrated. Somehow, acknowledging and coming clean to Eleanor about how my behavior affected *her* made me face my behavior in a new way. In other words, my new automatic response to being late hasn't just improved my relationship with Eleanor; it's improved my behavior too.

That's the power of a productive habit.

But changing our habits is not easy to do. Our intuitive responses are, well, intuitive. They're habits that feel natural and are hard to break. Even if they don't work, relying on them is what we know. In the heat of the moment, it's how we react. Knowing a new, effective, automatic response is half the battle. The other half is using it under stress. I've written *Four Seconds* to help you win both halves.

In part 1, "Change Your Mental Defaults," you will learn how to regain control of your behaviors and actions—in the short term and the long term—that serve your best interests, draw you toward your objectives, and make you happy. You will learn how to master your impulses and temptations. You will become calmer and more peaceful. The advice in part 1 will help you become grounded.

In part 2, "Strengthen Your Relationships," you will increase your capacity to handle difficult emotions—your own and other people's—and you will become a master at reacting and responding productively to difficult conversations and situations. The advice in part 2 will help you become connected to the people around you.

In part 3, "Optimize Your Work Habits," you will learn to work—and lead—in a way that inspires the motivation, loyalty, and commitment of the people around you. You'll subvert any tendencies that end up alienating colleagues or instigating opposition; instead, you'll encourage self-motivation, positivity, and support in your organization. The advice in part 3 will help you lead courageously, authentically, and with impact.

My hope is that *Four Seconds* will help you overcome your self-defeating habits and behaviors. While your counter-productive impulses may not disappear completely, I hope the advice in the pages that follow will help you gain power over them and help you develop new habits that advance your true interests, that help you make the impact you intend to make. The amount of time you will save by making better choices will be immeasurable. The positive impact you will have—on your life, your relationships, and your work—will be invaluable.

I can only assume that the guy with the gum on the bottom of his shoe hasn't yet noticed. He's probably still leaving a bright blue sticky trail in his wake. But you don't have to.

PART ONE

# Change Your Mental Defaults

t wasn't easy getting into my writing chair. The obstacles weren't physical—I was perfectly *able* to sit down and write. The obstacles—like most obstacles that distract us from achieving the things that are important to us—were mental.

I was busy, with lots of urgent things to get done, so sitting to write felt almost indulgent. The challenge of writing always invites procrastination even in the best of circumstances, but this morning I had been moving at a furious pace and was stressed about a client issue, both of which were in conflict with the slow, thoughtful pace that writing demands.

But, against all odds, there I was, finally settled into my writing.

I had just written my first sentence, when the door suddenly flew open and my daughter Sophia, who was seven years old at the time, rushed in.

"The kitchen is flooded!" she yelled. "Help!"

Seriously? Apparently, Daniel, who was five years old, filled a glass of water and neglected to turn off the tap. Oops.

My knee-jerk reaction was to yell at both Daniel and Sophia. I could feel energy surge in my body as my muscles tensed. In that moment, yelling felt both justified and appropriate.

But I paused and took a breath. Four seconds.

That breath was the hardest thing I did all day. In concept, breathing is easy. But pausing for a few seconds to take a breath in the midst of the swirling emotions I was feeling? When I was frustrated and mad and tired and worried? Not so easy.

Those four seconds—and the presence of mind to take them—are the first step to subverting our counter-productive knee-jerk reactions: the first step to making the smartest choice in the moment.

In part 1, you will learn to slow down—to create space between what you feel and what you do—and to make smarter snap decisions that move you toward the outcomes you desire. The chapters that follow will help you find that space, solidify it, and notice what happens in it. But more important, it will help you ditch your self-defeating mental habits that get in your way and replace them with productive ones. You will discover things like

- how indulging temptation is the key to overcoming it;

- why setting goals can actually derail performance;

- how strategic *dis*engagement can recover your focus and willpower;

- how doing nothing at all can solve the most difficult problems; and

- why most of our stress is caused by events of minimal consequence and how changing our expectations—not external reality—is the key to success.

I hope the advice in the following chapters helps you better master your impulses and temptations and adopt mental habits that lead to a productive, calmer, and more peaceful life.

# 1 Four Seconds

## Pause. Breathe.
## Course Correct.

THIS MORNING, LIKE EVERY MORNING, I SAT CROSS-LEGGED ON A cushion on the floor, rested my hands on my knees, closed my eyes, and did nothing but breathe for twenty minutes.

People say the hardest part about meditating is finding the time to meditate, which makes sense. Who these days has time to do nothing? It's hard to justify.

Meditation brings many benefits: it refreshes us, helps us settle into what's happening now, makes us wiser and gentler, helps us cope in a world that overloads us with information and communication, and more. But if you're still looking for a business case to justify spending time meditating, try this one: meditation makes you more productive.

How? By increasing your capacity to resist distracting urges.

Research shows that an ability to resist urges will improve your relationships, increase your dependability, and raise your performance.[1] If you can resist your urges, you can make better, more thoughtful decisions. You can be more intentional about what you say and how you say it. You can think about the outcome of your actions before following through on them.

Our ability to resist an impulse determines our success in learning a new behavior or changing an old habit. It's probably the single most important skill for our growth and development.

As it turns out, that's one of the things meditation teaches us. It's also one of the hardest to learn.

When I sat down to meditate this morning, relaxing a little more with each exhale, my concerns drifted away. My mind was truly empty of everything that had concerned it before I started meditating. Everything except the flow of my breath. My body felt blissful, and I was at peace.

For about four seconds.

That's how long it takes to take one breath. And within one breath, thoughts came flooding in. I felt an itch on my face and wanted to scratch it. A great title for my next book popped into my head, and I wanted to write it down before I forgot it. I thought of at least four phone calls I wanted to make and one difficult conversation I was going to have later that day. I became anxious, knowing I only had a few hours of writing time. What was I doing just sitting here? I wanted to open my eyes and look at how much time was left on my countdown timer. I heard my kids fighting in the other room and wanted to intervene.

Here's the key though: I wanted to do all those things, but I didn't do them. Instead, every time I had one of those thoughts, I brought my attention back to my breath.

Because, while four seconds is all it takes to lose focus, that's all it takes to regain focus too. Four seconds—one breath—is all it takes to stop yourself from a counter-productive knee-jerk re-action. And four seconds is all it takes to make a more inten-tional, strategic choice that's more likely to get you where you want to go.

Sometimes, *not* following through on something you *want to do* is a problem, like not writing that proposal you've been procrastinating about or not having that difficult conversation you've been avoiding.

But other times, the problem is that you *do* follow through on something you *don't want to do,* like speaking instead of listening or playing politics instead of rising above them.

Meditation teaches us to resist the urge of that counterproductive follow-through.

Later in this book, I will suggest that it's easier and more reliable to create an environment that supports your goals than it is to depend on willpower, but sometimes you do need to rely on plain, old-fashioned, self-control.

For example, self-control is useful when an employee makes a mistake and you want to yell at him even though you know that it's better—for him and for the morale of the group—to ask some questions and discuss it gently and rationally. Or when you want to blurt something out in a meeting but know you'd be better off listening. Or when you want to buy or sell a stock based on your emotions even though the fundamentals and your research suggest a different action. Or when you want to check e-mail every three minutes instead of focusing on the task at hand.

Each time you meditate, you will be proving to yourself that temptation is only a suggestion. You are in control.

Does that mean you never follow an urge? Of course not. Urges hold useful information. If you're hungry, it may be a good indication that you need to eat. But it also may be an indication that you're bored or struggling with a difficult piece of work. Meditation gives you practice having power over your urges so you can make intentional choices about which to follow and which to let pass.

So how do you do it? If you're just starting, keep it very simple.

Sit with your back straight enough that your breathing is comfortable—on a chair or a cushion on the floor—and set a timer for however many minutes you want to meditate. Once you start the timer, close your eyes, relax, and don't move except to breathe, until the timer goes off. Focus on your breath going in and out. Every time you have a thought or an urge, notice it and bring yourself back to your breath.

That's it. Simple but challenging. Try it—today—for five minutes. And then try it again tomorrow.

And if you don't have five minutes? Then try it for four seconds.

> A four-second pause—the time it takes to take one breath in, one breath out—can be powerful enough to subvert a poor decision and replace it with a smarter one.

● ● ● ●

# 2 Why the Pinto Blew Up

## Rethink Goal Setting

"SOPHIA! DANIEL! ISABELLE!" I YELLED ACROSS THE APARTMENT AT my three children who were playing together in their bedroom. "The school bus arrives in ten minutes. Let's see who can brush their teeth and get to the door first."

They dashed toward the bathroom, giggling. Two minutes later, Daniel had won with Sophia in close second, and Isabelle right after her. I smiled at my own victory. I had achieved my goal of getting them to the door with their teeth brushed in record time.

Or did I?

Yes, they were at the door in time. But two minutes from start to finish meant that they didn't brush their teeth very well, they definitely didn't floss, and the bathroom was a mess.

We all know how important it is to have goals, right? And not just any goals, but stretch goals. Big Hairy Audacious Goals (or BHAGs, as they're known to the inner goal-setting crowd).

It makes sense: if you don't know specifically where you're going, then you'll never get there. And if you don't set the bar high enough, you'll never live up to your potential.

Goal setting is accepted common sense in the business world, and it's reinforced by research. Like that study done on the 1979 class in the Harvard MBA program, which you may have heard of: Only 3 percent of the graduating students wrote down clear goals. Ten years later, those 3 percent were worth ten times the worth of the rest of the class combined. Compelling, right?

It would be if it were true. But it isn't. That study doesn't exist. It's pure urban myth.

Still, that's just one specious story. Questioning the wisdom of setting stretch goals is like questioning the very foundation of business. We might debate which goals to set, or how to set them, but who would debate whether to set goals at all?

I'd like to.

It's not that goals, by their nature, are bad. It's just that they come with a number of side effects that suggest you may be better off without them.

The authors of a Harvard Business School working paper, "Goals Gone Wild,"[2] reviewed a number of research studies related to goals and concluded that the upside of goal setting has been exaggerated, and the downside, the "systematic harm caused by goal setting," has been disregarded.

They identified clear side effects associated with goal setting, including "a narrow focus that neglects non-goal areas, a rise in unethical behavior, distorted risk preferences, corrosion of organizational culture, and reduced intrinsic motivation."

Here are two examples of goals gone wild the authors described in their paper:

- Sears set a productivity goal for their auto-repair staff of bringing in $147 for every hour of work. Did this motivate employees? Sure. It motivated them to overcharge on a companywide basis.

- Remember the Ford Pinto? A car that ignited when it was rear-ended? The Pinto resulted in fifty-three deaths and many more injuries because workers omitted safety checks in pursuit of Lee Iacocca's BHAG goal of a car that would be "under 2,000 pounds and under $2,000" by 1970.

And here's another via the *New York Times*:[3]

- Ken O'Brien, the former New York Jets quarterback, was throwing too many interceptions. So he was given what seemed to be a pretty reasonable goal—fewer interceptions thrown—and penalized financially for every one. It worked. He threw fewer interceptions. But only because he threw fewer passes. His overall performance suffered.

It's practically impossible to predict the negative side effects of a goal.

When we set goals, we're taught to make them specific and measurable and time bound. However, it turns out that those characteristics are precisely the reasons goals can backfire. A specific, measurable, time-bound goal drives behavior that's narrowly focused and often leads to either cheating or myopia. Yes, we often reach the goal. But at what cost?

So what can you do in the absence of goals? It's still often necessary to drive toward achievements, especially in business. We need help setting direction and measuring progress. But maybe there's a better way to achieve those things while sidestepping a goal's negative side effects.

I want to propose one approach: instead of identifying goals, consider identifying areas of focus.

A goal defines an outcome you want to achieve; an area of focus establishes activities you want to spend your time doing. A goal is a result; an area of focus is a path. A goal points to a future you intend to reach; an area of focus settles you into the present.

A sales goal, for example, might name a revenue target or a specific number of new clients won. An operations goal might articulate a cost savings.

An area of focus in sales, on the other hand, might involve having lots of conversations with appropriate prospects. An operations area of focus might identify areas you want to explore for cost savings.

Obviously, these aren't mutually exclusive. You could have a goal and an area of focus. In fact, one could argue that you need both together—the goal specifies where you're going, and the area of focus describes how you plan to get there.

But there is a benefit to concentrating on an area of focus without a goal.

An area of focus taps into your intrinsic motivation, offers no stimulus or incentive to cheat or take unnecessary risks, leaves every positive possibility and opportunity open, and encourages collaboration while reducing corrosive competition—all while moving forward on the things you and your organization value most.

In other words, an area of focus offers all the advantages of a goal without the negative side effects.

How do you do it? It's simple: identify the things you want to spend your time doing—or the things that you and your manager decide are the most valuable use of your time—and spend your time doing those things. The rest takes care of itself. I have found that five major areas of focus are about the limit before your efforts get diluted.

The key is to resist the temptation to identify the outcome you want to achieve. Leave that open and allow yourself to be pleasantly surprised. I'm not suggesting that this is easy to do. I never realized how goal focused I was until I tried to stop focusing on goals. Without goals, I found it hard to trust that anything would get done at all.

But things got done. And in my experience, not only will you achieve at least as much as you would have if you had set goals, but you'll enjoy the process far more, avoiding unnecessary stress and temptation.

In other words, if we focus on the tasks instead of the outcome, my kids will still get to the door on time, but they will have flossed, brushed thoroughly, and left the bathroom clean too.

> Setting goals isn't always a beneficial habit. Identify and spend your time on areas of focus instead and you'll get where you want to go more effectively.

• • • •

# 3  Byron's Real Problem

## Commit to
## Following Through

"PETER," MY FRIEND BYRON E-MAILED ME A FEW DAYS AGO. "I HAV-
en't been diligent about working out over the past five years and
I'm trying to get back in the gym and get myself into a healthier
state. I've found that on my quest for a Mind, Body, Spirit balance, my body has been neglected. I need to fix it, and it's VERY
hard for me to get motivated. Any insight?"

Something you should know about Byron is that he recently
started a business, and he's constantly developing his skills
through training programs he pays for with his own money. So
it's not that Byron is unmotivated in general. It's just that he
thinks he's unmotivated to work out.

But Byron is wrong. "I need to fix it," he wrote. He *is* motivated to work out; otherwise he wouldn't have e-mailed me. He
clearly cares about getting fit, and when you care about something, you're motivated.

No, Byron's challenge isn't motivation. It's follow-through.

It's important to realize this distinction because as long as
Byron thinks he's solving a motivation problem, he'll be looking
for the wrong solution. He'll try to get himself excited. He'll re-

mind himself that being in shape is really important. Maybe he'll visualize the partners he'll attract if he looks better or the years he'll add to his life if he gets in better shape.

Each attempt to motivate himself will only increase his stress and guilt as it widens the gap between his motivation and his follow-through, between how badly he wants to work out and his failure to do so. We have a misconception that if we only cared enough about something, we would do something about it. But that's not true.

Motivation is in the mind; follow-through is in the practice. Motivation is conceptual; follow-through is practical. In fact, the solution to a motivation problem is the exact opposite of the solution to a follow-through problem. The mind is essential to motivation. But with follow-through, it's the mind that gets in the way.

We've all experienced our mind sabotaging our aspirations. We decide to go to the gym after work, but then, when it comes time to go, we think, *It's late. I'm tired. Maybe I'll skip it today.* We decide we want to meditate, but then, we look at our watch and decide, *I don't have the time.* We decide we need to be more supportive of our employees, but then, when someone makes a mistake, we think, *If I don't make a big deal about this, he's going to do it again.* We decide we need to speak more in meetings, but then, when we're sitting in the meeting, we think, *I'm not sure what I'm going to say really adds value.*

Here's the key: if you want to follow through on something, stop thinking. Shut down the sabotaging conversation that goes on in your head before it starts. Don't take the bait. Stop arguing with yourself. Make a very specific decision about something you want to do and don't question it. By very specific, I mean decisions like these: "I will work out tomorrow at 6:00 A.M.," or "I will meditate for fifteen minutes as soon as I wake up," or "I only point out the things my employee does right," or "I will say at least one thing in the next meeting."

Then, when your mind starts to argue with you—and I guarantee it will—ignore it. You're smarter than your mind. You can see right through it.

I once took a golf lesson with a pro who taught me a certain way to swing the club. After the lesson, he issued a warning.

"When you play with others, some people will want to give you advice. Just listen to them politely, thank them for their advice, and then completely ignore it and do exactly what I've just told you to do."

That, Byron, is precisely how you should respond to your mind.

> If you are having trouble accomplishing a task or activity, the culprit might be follow-through. Rather than motivating yourself with an internal pep talk, shut down your mind: decide on a specific action or task, and don't allow your internal thoughts to talk you out of it.

● ● ● ●

# 4 My First TEDx Talk

## Ditch the Urge
## to Be Perfect

"UGH!" I PUT MY HANDS ON MY HEAD AND LOOKED AWAY FROM MY computer at the ceiling. "I can't do this! It's just not coming out right!"

Eleanor looked over sympathetically from the desk next to mine; she knew how hard I had been working. I was preparing for a TEDx Talk I was scheduled to give in Flint, Michigan, and although I was somewhere around version 25 of my speech, I was still dissatisfied.

I love the idea behind TED: you have eighteen minutes to talk about an idea worth sharing. Lots of well-known people have given fascinating talks, and I felt honored to be invited to offer mine. I also felt tremendous pressure to make it a great speech.

I had been asked to focus on the topic of learning: a good thing because I have lots to say, but a bad thing because I have lots to say. If I had been given eight hours to speak, I could have done it off the cuff. But eighteen minutes? Which one of my ideas is important enough, interesting enough, and matters to me enough to choose? And once I chose one, how should I present it so it's engaging, funny, clever, clear, and creative? All in eighteen minutes?

On top of that, every TED speaker is videotaped, with three cameras, and the talks are posted on the web. This is wonderful if my talk goes well. But if it doesn't? If it's a disaster? There will be no escape. I wanted it to be perfect. So I had cordoned off a significant amount of time over several weeks to write and practice my talk.

I should know better. When I try to make something perfect, it's almost a guarantee that I'll overthink it, which means I'll spend too much time spinning with too little progress. Hence version 25.

On some level, overthinking is part of the process of taking on bigger challenges. But overthinking is rarely helpful, increases stress, takes a tremendous amount of time, and never produces a better product.

I cleared my schedule for two weeks so I could focus completely on the speech—a big mistake.

While it takes a lot of time to work on something creative, it can't be accomplished all at once. Creativity needs to percolate over time. After a few focused hours in a day, my productivity declined rapidly.

So what happened to all those hours I had cordoned off to focus on the speech? I couldn't possibly spend them all *working* on the speech. But, it turns out, I could spend a surprising amount of them *stressing* about the speech.

Why didn't I spend my time on other important tasks? This doesn't make rational sense, but I think, somehow, that would have been an acknowledgment that I wasn't spending my time where I thought I should have been: working on the speech. So, instead of doing valuable work, I took long breaks, distracting myself with the Internet and food. Crazy, but there you have it.

Others tried to support me by telling me not to worry—that I'm a natural at it, and I would be great. I give speeches all the time, and I should just do what I always do: be myself.

But those thoughts just increased the pressure because they reminded me of the expectation that the speech be really, really great.

So what should we do when we're under pressure to deliver on a big challenge?

For me, two things were most helpful:

## 1. I ran out of time.

I had two weeks, then one week, then three days. That's when my productivity kicked up. There's a saying: if you want something done, ask a busy person to do it. Another way to think about it: if you want to get something done, become a busy person. Don't empty your schedule, fill it. The busier you are, the less time you have to get in your own way. I should have cordoned off a few hours each day and filled everything else with work I considered important.

## 2. I changed my expectations.

One morning, a few days before the speech, I found a note on my computer, left by Eleanor. She told me the speech might *not* end up being that great, but in the big picture, it wouldn't make a huge difference. Surely it would be good. And if not that, then at least okay. Which, ultimately, would be just fine. Once I read that, something shifted in me. I stopped trying so hard. I stopped trying to be funny, smart, clever, or creative. I stopped trying to talk about the three most important things. I stopped trying to make this my best talk ever. Instead, I set a goal I knew I could achieve: talk about one thing—not necessarily *the* thing, just something that was meaningful to me—and talk about it simply and passionately.

Life is a process, and while one stellar moment—be it a success or a failure—can make a difference, it's far more likely that the steady production of many adequate moments over a significant period of time will make a much bigger difference.

> To get your most important things done without losing your mind, stop trying so hard and aiming for perfection. Instead, try racing as quickly as you can through the next phase of work. Spending less time on it might just make it better.

• • • •

# 5   It Finally Felt Like Mine

## Trust Yourself First

LAST WEEK, I ATTENDED AN EVENING EVENT TO HONOR AND ADVANCE the vision of the late Dr. Allan Rosenfield, Dean of Columbia's Mailman School of Public Health for twenty-two years. Allan was a giant in global health, dedicated in particular to women's reproductive health and rights.

There was a long slate of estimable speakers, but as the evening wore on, I began to lose attention. Then Hoosen (Jerry) Coovadia, a professor at the University of KwaZulu-Natal, South Africa, stepped up to the lectern.

He looked at the audience, and without fanfare, put aside his speech. "Most of what I planned to say has already been said," he told us.

Then, instead of reading his prepared remarks, he spent a few minutes talking, off the cuff, about Allan's uncommon ability to "see in the dark"—to see injustices that the rest of us overlooked—and take action.

Of the many speeches that night, his talk, unscripted, simple, heartfelt, is the one that affected me the most.

Jerry modeled what Allan lived: he saw in the dark. The evening didn't need another eloquent, grandiose speech about the state of global health. Jerry let go of all his hard preparation in favor of what he saw was best in the moment. His ability to notice the need, pause, and spin on a dime was remarkable. It showed flexibility, presence, and focus, but also something deeper: it showed trust in himself.

In the last chapter, I shared how I overworked, overthought, and overprepared my first TEDx Talk on learning.

Each time I created a new version, I sent it out to trusted friends—smart, generous, insightful people—and asked for their advice and direction. Was it interesting enough? Clear enough? Creative enough? Funny enough?

Yet each time they came back with their valuable, thoughtful feedback, I became a little more lost and a little less sure of my message, my ideas, and myself.

It's not that I had a hard time hearing criticism. It was the opposite: I was too quick to incorporate it, too eager to please, too willing to change in order to get the right response.

Many of us have spent our lives listening to our parents, teachers, managers, and leaders. Choosing what we are told to choose. Being told gently who we are. Molding ourselves to the feedback of others. Seeking approval. Reaching for recognition.

There is good reason to learn from the wisdom of others. But there is also a cost: as we shape ourselves to the desires, preferences, and expectations of others, we risk losing ourselves. We can become frozen without their direction, unable to make our own choices, lacking trust in our own insights.

There is a simple remedy to the insecurity of being ourselves: stop asking.

Instead, take the time, and the quiet, to decide what you think. That is how we find the part of ourselves we gave up. That is how we become powerful, clever, creative, and insightful. That is how we gain our sight.

After becoming distracted by the feedback I was getting, after Eleanor suggested I was trying too hard, after I ran out of time to make five more revisions, I finally did what Jerry did: I put the speech aside and made very personal choices about what I wanted to share.

How did I arrive at those choices? I looked through the thousands of words I had written in preparation for the talk to find something I felt added my unique perspective to the conversation about learning. It seems obvious to me now, but how could I have hoped to find my unique perspective by asking others? Instead, I looked into the dark for what others had overlooked.

This trusting of yourself is not just about writing a speech. It's about speaking in meetings. It's about choosing projects to pursue. It's about advocating for budgets. It's about having the courage to do work that moves you. Can you trust yourself enough to follow your own impulses?

Once I decided to stop asking others what they thought about what I thought, I noticed something interesting: I try harder when I'm not relying on others. I fix things I might otherwise leave for others to fix. I work more diligently to ensure my perspective holds together.

In the past, when I sent someone an article for comments, knowing it needed some work, I was being lazy. And my laziness, enabled by the generosity of others, had the side effect of reducing my faith in my abilities to work through the places I got stuck.

I am not suggesting we ignore feedback. It's useful to know how others react to our work. After my complete rewrite, I performed the speech several times to different audiences as practice.

But this time, I didn't ask them to assess my message. I asked them to assess my delivery. What did they get from my talk? Did I convey my message in a way that communicated my passion for it?

And when I finally gave my speech in Flint, Michigan, it felt clear, focused, and authentic.

It felt like mine.

> Next time you feel insecure about a task or project and are about to reach out for feedback and approval, ask yourself what you think first. Take some quiet time to listen to yourself and trust your mind and heart. It often helps not to think about what others think.

● ● ● ●

# 6 Nothing Helped My Tennis Elbow

## Stand Back and Do Nothing

I'D HAD TENDONITIS IN MY ELBOW FOR OVER A YEAR. EVEN SOME-thing as gentle as twisting a doorknob made me wince in pain. I went to see my brother, Bertie, who also happens to be my doctor.

As Bertie examined my elbow, I reminded him of everything I had done to try to fix my problem. When it began to hurt, I used ibuprofen. When that didn't work, we tried two injections of cortisone, six months apart. Meanwhile, I did physical therapy, tried ultrasound, used a brace, performed daily exercises, applied ice, and went to acupuncture and massage. Pushed to the edge, I even did an experimental therapy—a platelet-rich plasma injection, which had gained media attention because some high-profile athletes had used it. The shot was incredibly painful and only made my problem worse.

"Nothing has helped!" I complained.

"I have an idea," Bertie said. "Something we haven't yet tried."

"What?" I hoped it wouldn't be too time-consuming or expensive.

"You just said it yourself," he replied. "Nothing."

He suggested I stop all treatments for the next six months. "All your attempts to fix your elbow might just be agitating it," he told me. "I bet after a few months of doing nothing the pain will just go away."

I was skeptical but game. Sure enough, within a few months, my pain had disappeared.

In some situations, doing nothing—forever—is the right response. With my tendonitis, doing nothing helped. Sometimes, not trying to fix something is precisely what's needed to fix it.

It's a hard strategy to follow because we have a penchant for being proactive. If there's a problem, we feel better when we attack it aggressively. But consider the idea that we might spend a lot of time, effort, and money solving problems that can't, in fact, be solved with time, effort, and money.

In 2009 Americans spent about $3.6 billion on over-the-counter cold, cough, and throat remedies, according to the *New York Times*.[4] And yet, the article concluded, there's very little evidence that any of those medicines do anything to cure, or even shorten the duration of, a cold. And some remedies, like taking antibiotics, bring along side effects that risk making some people worse.

In other words, the best strategy for coping with the common cold is to do nothing.

Does this strategy apply outside medicine? There's a lot of talk these days about creating new businesses through incentives. Does the money and effort put into incentives help? According to a study released by the Kauffman Foundation,[5] the answer is no.

Data from the U.S. Census Bureau indicates that the number of new businesses started each year between 1977 and 2005 varied only by 3–6 percent. According to the study, "none of the factors that might bear on prospective entrepreneurs' decisions to form new companies—recessions, expansions, tax changes, population growth, scarce or abundant capital, technological advances or others—has much impact on the pace of U.S. startups."

In other words, the best strategy for stimulating new business creation is to do nothing.

How about interpersonal relationships? Some time ago, I had a falling out with someone close to me. I tried several times to address it—I sent e-mails, made phone calls, and even sent a gift—but nothing I did left either of us feeling any better. Eventually, I gave up and wrote the person off. For a long time, I did nothing. Recently, I saw this person again and, somehow, it felt like that falling out was behind us. Well, mostly. It wasn't as nice as it had been before the falling out. But it was a lot better than when we were trying to actively work it out.

I'm not suggesting we address all problems by doing nothing. Often addressing something head-on is precisely what's needed. It can be incredibly effective to bring something up that's been simmering in the background and deal with it openly. I'm a huge fan of discussing "undiscussables," and I've seen it work wonders.

But how many unnecessary arguments could have been avoided by brushing off something unimportant? Perhaps we could have allowed someone's weakness to go unmentioned. Maybe we could have forgiven without requiring an act of contrition. In other words, sometimes, the best strategy for working out a difficult interpersonal issue is to do nothing.

So how do we know whether to do something or nothing?

"When many cures are offered for a disease," wrote Anton Chekhov, "it means the disease is not curable." If past experience or data suggests that multiple solutions are possible but none are reliably successful, nothing may be the best strategy.

Also, if you've tried two or three solutions and none of them have worked, perhaps it's time to try nothing.

It's been several years since my elbow stopped hurting. But I'm superstitious and, quite frankly, a little worried that writing this—declaring so brashly that I conquered my tendonitis by doing nothing—will somehow start the pain again.

I hope that doesn't happen. But if it does, at least now I know what I'm going to do: nothing.

> Resist the temptation to fix everything. Sometimes, doing nothing at all works better than doing something.

• • • •

# 7 Everything Is Amazing and No One Is Happy

## Accept Reality.
## Change Expectations.

IMAGINE YOU'RE SAILING IN THE BAHAMAS, SIPPING A COLD DRINK and listening to the water lapping the sides of the boat.

Relaxing, right? Not for my friend Rob.

Rob is not usually stressed-out. For many people, Rob's daily work would be hair-pulling stressful—he's a real estate developer who routinely deals with a multitude of nagging problems related to renters, banks, lawsuits, property management, and rapidly changing valuations. But Rob routinely handles it all with steadiness and perspective.

So why was he stressed that blissful day on his boat? The same reason most of us get stressed: frustrated expectations. Rob had an important call to make, and his cell phone wasn't working. He was experiencing the gap between what he expected to happen and what was actually happening.

That's the underlying cause of stress, and it's afflicting us more these days than ever because our expectations keep rising, thanks in part to exponential improvements in our technology.

In a hilarious interview with Conan O'Brien,[6] the comedian Louis C.K. talked about how everything is amazing right now and nobody's happy. He tells the story of being on a plane and, for the first time, experiencing working Internet at thirty thousand feet. He was amazed. The person in the seat next to him was also surfing the web happily until the connection dropped. The man immediately threw his arms up in the air and yelled, "This is bullshit!"

"How quickly the world owes him something he knew existed only ten seconds ago," Louis C.K. said. I fall into this trap, and most people around me do too. We expect more not only from our technology, but from each other and from ourselves.

Rob is usually laid-back in the face of his ever-present problems precisely because they're ever-present. He expects them. Renters always have complaints. Banks always want more information. Lawsuits happen. Valuations always change. These things are routine, and he has routine responses to them, so they don't stress him out.

But that day on his boat, Rob was expecting his cell to work. So the cell outage far from land, where there's no alternative means of communicating his absence on an important phone call created a stressful unmet expectation.

So what can you do about the stress and frustration that comes from unmet expectations? You have two choices: either change the reality around you, or change your expectations.

Sometimes it's possible to change reality. Continuously frustrated with an employee? Try helping him improve his competence. If that doesn't work, you can fire him.

But often the reality around you is difficult to change. What if it's a peer with whom you're frustrated? Or maybe an entire department? You can't fire them all. Maybe you can stop working with them, but that's probably not in your control. You could quit, but that brings with it a host of new stress.

In my experience, trying to change reality isn't usually a stress *reliever;* it's a stress *creator.* A small thing—like changing my seat on an airplane—can be such a pain that even if it works it's often not worth the struggle. And the bigger things—like getting more done in a day—can be even more frustrating. That last example is especially frustrating because it's an expectation I have of myself, so I really believe it should be in my control.

And so I've come to believe the best strategy for reducing stress is to change your expectations.

In other words, get used to not getting what you want. I know this isn't consistent with the kind of go-get-'em attitude most of us have been taught to embrace. But most of the time, fighting reality is not worth the effort. Either you can't change what's around you, or the fight is more stressful than the reward.

If changing your expectations proves too hard, your next best move is to get some perspective.

Imagine a scale from one through ten, with ten being the worst reality you can imagine—something like living in a war zone or being in the World Trade Center on 9/11. Maybe nine is a serious illness that most probably will result in death. Perhaps eight is something that will forever alter your life, like going to jail or an accident that puts you in a wheelchair. Let's say seven is something that temporarily alters your life, like losing your job or having to move out of a home you can no longer afford.

Do you see where I'm going with this?

Almost everything we freak out about is somewhere in the one-to-two range of dashed expectations. In other words, our moods and our stress levels are determined by events that actually matter remarkably little.

That's useful to remember when you find yourself utterly irritated at your cable company because they erroneously added five dollars to your bill and then keep you on hold for thirty minutes while they investigate the matter. Or when a direct report gives you work you consider sloppy. I'm not saying don't correct the work. I'm simply suggesting it may not be worth getting worked up about.

That's not always easy. A number of small stressors add up to a lot of stress, and it's natural to be stressed by things that don't really matter in the whole scheme of things. I do it all the time.

We can substantially reduce our stress by recognizing that in many situations, we have become perfectionists in realms where perfection isn't necessary, realistic, or even useful.

Rob's stress was highest when he thought the problem was just with *his* cell phone. But, eventually, he found out that there was a cell outage throughout the Bahamas. Somehow, that helped him change his expectations. He knew there was nothing he could do.

Once he was able to get some perspective, he settled into his new reality. Where was missing that call on the scale from one to ten? No more than a one.

And just like that, no cell service for twelve hours turned into a real vacation.

> If you can't change reality—and usually you can't—then look carefully to see it for what it is. Once your perspective changes, so does your ability to respond strategically and productively to the world around you.

• • • •

# 8 The Value of Drinking Tea

## Make Time for Rituals

I RECENTLY SAW THE MOVIE *THE LAST SAMURAI* FOR THE SECOND time. Set in Japan in the 1870s, it tells the story of an American Civil War veteran who was captured by samurai fighters and, over time, learned to honor their ways.

The first time I saw the movie, when it came out in 2003, I was enthralled by the beautifully choreographed fight scenes. But this time, I was most moved by a scene I don't even remember seeing the first time: a samurai drinking tea.

Sitting at a low table, the samurai moved deliberately, singularly focused on his tea. He contemplated it. Then poured it. Then sipped it, tasted it, and finally, swallowed it.

This, I realized, was the source of the samurai's strength.

His acrobatics were impressive, but they were merely a *demonstration* of his strength. The *source* was this tea ritual and many other rituals like it. His power as a warrior came from his patience, precision, attention to subtlety, concentration, and his reverence for the moment.

The power of ritual is profound and underappreciated. Mostly, I think, it's because we live in a time-starved culture in which ritual is time indulgent. Who can afford the luxury of doing one thing at a time? Who has the patience to pause and honor an activity before and after we do it?

We all should.

Religions understand and leverage the power of ritual. In Judaism, blessings are as plentiful as iPhone apps. Waking up? There's a blessing for that. Washing your hands? Experiencing something new? Eating a meal? There's a blessing for each one. Every religion I know has similar practices to make our experience of the world sacred.

That might be why we avoid ritual in the business world. Religion is so loaded, so personal. But ritual doesn't have to be religious; it's just a tool used in religions. Rituals are about paying attention. They're about stopping for a moment and noticing what you're about to do, what you've just done, or both. They're about making the most of a particular moment. And that's something we could use a lot more of in the business world.

Imagine if we started each meeting by recognizing the power of collaboration and then dedicated ourselves, without distraction, to the meeting's areas of focus—perhaps even acknowledging that each person's views, ambitions, and priorities are important and need to be heard.

What if every performance review began with a short thought about the importance of clear and open communication? If every time we worked on a spreadsheet someone else created for us, we paused to acknowledge the complexity of the work she did and the attention to detail she brought to it? If at the beginning of the day we paused to honor the work we are about to do and the people with whom we are about to do it?

Here's what makes it easy to get started with this: no one needs to know.

Start with just yourself. Sit at your desk in the morning, pause before booting up your computer, and mark the moment. Do this by taking a deep breath. Or by arranging your pens. Whatever it is, do it with the intention of creating respect for what you're about to begin. Do the same before you make a phone call. Or receive one. Or before you meet with a colleague or customer.

Each time we pause, notice, and offer respect for an activity, it reminds us to appreciate and focus on what we're about to do. And by elevating each activity, we'll take it more seriously. We'll get more pleasure from it. The people with whom we work will feel more respected. And we'll feel more self-respect. Which means we'll work better with each other and produce better results.

That focus will help us accomplish our tasks more carefully, more proficiently, and more productively. And all the research shows that that kind of singular focus will make us far more efficient.

In other words, that time-indulgent ritual thing? It might just be the perfect antidote to a time-starved world.

> Stop going through the motions. Take a moment before each task to consider, focus on, and appreciate what you are about to do. That kind of ritualized attention isn't just powerful and productive, it's pleasurable too.

• • • •

# 9 Before Slipping the Kayak into the Water

## Prepare Every Day

MY WIFE ELEANOR AND I WERE ALONE ON A THREE-WEEK KAYAK expedition in Prince William Sound in Alaska. Eleanor was in college; I had just graduated. We had spent plenty of time in the wilderness but never just the two of us—and never this kind of wilderness. When we landed in Anchorage, I looked around for a currency-exchange desk before Eleanor reminded me we were still in the United States.

Prior to arriving, we prepared meticulously, studying the nautical charts, plotting our route, and practicing our kayaking skills. We paddled into the nastiest surf we could find and then rolled ourselves upside down to see how quickly we could either roll back over or get back in the kayak if we came out. In Prince William Sound, there's no margin for error. You can survive in the freezing water only four to five minutes.

Now that we were on Prince William Sound, we were thankful for all our preparations. And knowing how quickly the weather changes in Alaska, we had a ritual of precautions we took every morning before pushing the boat off the relative safety of the beach. We carefully packed everything in waterproof bags and placed those bags in the watertight compartments in our boat. We kept all our essentials—VHF radio, sunblock, signal mirror, peanut butter, and chocolate chips—the stuff we couldn't live without, in a dry bag in my kayak cockpit.

And every morning, before we left shore, we asked the same question: "If we died today, what mistake would *Sea Kayaker* magazine get us for?"

Before coming to Alaska, I read through the accident reports in every past issue of *Sea Kayaker* magazine I could get my hands on. The reports identified the mistakes and poor decisions people made that led, more often than I shared with my parents, to their deaths.

One person knew he shouldn't paddle that day because the weather was bad and the surf was rough, but he had a meeting to get to and didn't want to miss the ferry home. Well, he missed that ferry and every one since. Another kayaker, on the last day of his trip, didn't bother to pack his gear in waterproof bags since he didn't expect to need it. But then a wave hit his boat, and he flipped, and everything got wet. He got back to shore but had nothing to keep him warm, and eventually, he died of hypothermia. Then there was the Outward Bound course that found itself surprised by strong winds and currents off the coast of Baja California. Three of the students died.

So each morning, before pushing our kayaks away from shore, I stood there for a few minutes thinking about the day—our plan, the weather, our gear, pullout points, our skills, challenges we might encounter—and then I asked if we were prepared.

And now, years later, from the safety of my office chair, I still think that's the right mentality with which to approach each day.

We are all so busy. In the rush to accomplish more and more, how often do we jump into conversations or meetings or projects unprepared? It's our knee-jerk reaction to having a lot to do. Preparation time seems disposable, so we jump head first into situations and, as a result, make mistakes, take longer, and waste time.

The questions I ask myself today are slightly different from those Eleanor and I asked ourselves during our kayak trip because the risks are very different. But the idea is the same: are you prepared for this day? For the meetings you have planned? Have you really thought about the work you plan to do? Have you anticipated the risks that might take you off track? Are you focused on what you want to achieve? Will your plan for this day bring you one day closer to what you really want? Far from a waste of time, that kind of preparation is precisely what makes you productive.

In Alaska, we completed our trip successfully because we took the time to prepare for each day as if that day had been the most important day of our lives. Because, in fact, the risks were great enough that if we had not prepared that way, it might have been the most important day of our lives—the last one.

Why not treat today, given that it's the only day you've got right now, with the same importance?

> Beware of jumping into things without thinking them through. Each morning, make the time to ask yourself this question: "Am I prepared for this day?" You may still be ambushed, but you'll even be more prepared for that, just by asking the question.

• • • •

# 10 A Lesson from My Wireless Router

## Reset Yourself

MY WIRELESS CONNECTION TO THE INTERNET HAD SUDDENLY stopped working. At first I was frustrated. I had been in the middle of browsing some books on Amazon. But I quickly took it as a blessing. I had an article to write, and the Amazon browsing was a distraction. I resisted the temptation to distract myself further by trying to fix it and got to work. I finished the article in record time.

That's a lesson in itself. But it's not the whole story.

Once I was done with the article, I needed to send it to my editor. What was previously a distraction—fixing my Internet connection—was now essential. So I put all my deep technological know-how to work: I yelled at it.

No change. So I yelled at it some more. When that didn't work, I closed all the applications and rebooted the computer. It still didn't work. So I opened the wireless-router software and played with some of the settings. Still nothing. Finally, I turned the wireless router off and on several times, but that didn't do anything either.

I just sat there silently, angrily staring at my computer equipment, ready to admit defeat. But then I remembered the solution that had worked for me before, when all else failed. I unplugged everything and waited one minute. While everything was unplugged, I had nothing to do, so I just sat there.

It's strange, because one minute is so little, but when the time was up, I felt noticeably different. I wasn't angry or frustrated or annoyed. I wasn't on the verge—as I was before—of throwing away all my electronics if this solution didn't work. I felt oddly refreshed. My situation hadn't changed, but my perspective had.

It turns out that when I unplugged my equipment, I unplugged myself at the same time. And when that short, barely noticeable minute had passed, I felt different. Renewed. Ready to speak softly and gently to my wireless router instead of yelling at it. Maybe even joke around with it a bit to lighten up the tension.

Which got me thinking: this unplug-and-stop-everything-for-a-minute strategy might be a pretty good solution for whenever things aren't working in life.

That point was reinforced for me in a recent cell phone call I had with Eleanor while she was traveling. We were having a difficult conversation, and each of us had the feeling that the other one wasn't listening. Then the call was dropped. We tried calling each other back but only got voicemail. So we sat there for a minute, each of us in our respective places. Unplugged.

When we eventually connected again, the tone of the conversation changed radically. We were softer with each other. More attentive. More forgiving and loving. Better at listening and rephrasing what we heard the other one saying. I never thought I'd say this but, for once, I was happy that my cellular network is unreliable. It gave us both a minute to breathe and get some perspective.

Unplugging and waiting for a minute is an unexpected strategy because it appears passive. You aren't actively developing new strategies, arguments, or viewpoints. In fact, you aren't actively doing anything.

When you unplug and wait for a minute, you restore yourself to your factory-default settings, which for most of us tend to be generous, openhearted, creative, connected, and hopeful. That makes us more likely to be effective when we plug back in.

In a meeting that's going nowhere? Take a break. Making no headway on that proposal you need to write? Stand up and take a walk. Fighting with your kids? Give yourself a time-out. Unplug for a minute and breathe.

This is not a strategy that requires practice and skill building. All it requires is remembering to do it. Sometimes, life requires active, willful engagement. But sometimes, the smartest move is disengagement. That magic minute of not doing anything has the power to change just about everything.

Which is what happened with my great and wise teacher, my wireless router. Miracle of miracles, when I plugged it back in after that minute of waiting, my wireless Internet starting working again. And so did I.

> When you need to regain your balance—in a contentious conversation or a difficult situation—rather than build your momentum, do nothing for a minute, essentially giving yourself a time-out. Resetting yourself has the power to help you change your perspective.

• • • •

# 11 This Is What It Feels Like to . . .

## Stop Performing.
## Start Experiencing.

THE NIGHT BEFORE OUR WEDDING, ELEANOR AND I STOOD AWK-wardly in the center of a large room, surrounded by our family and our closest friends. There was no particular reason to be uncomfortable; this was just a rehearsal. Still, we were in the spotlight, and things weren't going smoothly. Neither the rabbi nor the cantor had arrived, and we didn't know where to stand, what to say, or what to do.

It had taken us eleven years—and a lot of work—to get to this point. Eleanor is Episcopalian, the daughter of a deacon, and I am Jewish, the son of a Holocaust survivor. The one thing our parents agreed upon before the wedding was that we shouldn't get married.

A friend of ours, Sue Anne Steffey Morrow, a Methodist minister, offered to stand in for the Jewish officiants who were absent. She moved us through the rehearsal, placing people in position, reading prayers, and lightening the mood with a few well-timed jokes.

When the rehearsal was over and we were feeling more relaxed, she offered me and Eleanor a piece of advice that remains one of the best I have ever received.

"Tomorrow hundreds of people will be watching you on the most important day of your life. Try to remember this: It's not a performance; it's an experience."

I love that she said, "Try to remember this." On the surface, it seems easy to remember, but in reality, it's almost impossible because much of what we do *feels* like a performance. We're graded in school and get performance reviews at work. We win races, earn titles, receive praise, and sometimes gain fame, all because of our performance. We're paid for our performance. Even little things—leading a meeting, having a hallway conversation, sending an e-mail—are followed by the silent but ever-present question, "How'd that go?"

In other words, we think life is a performance because, well, it kind of is. We feel judged by others because, often, we are. And let's be honest: it's not just they who judge us; most of us spend a considerable amount of energy judging others as well, which, of course, only reinforces our own experience of being judged and fuels our desire to perform.

But here's the paradox: living life as a performance is not only a recipe for stress and unhappiness; it also leads to mediocre performance. If you want to get better at anything, you need to experiment with an open mind, to try and fail, to willingly accept and learn from any outcome. And once you get an outcome you like, you need to be willing to shake it up again and try something different.

The best performers are lifelong learners, and the definition of a lifelong learner is someone who is constantly trying new things. That requires performing poorly much of the time and sometimes brilliantly, but often unpredictably so. If you view life as a performance, your failures will be so painful and terrifying that you will stop experimenting. But if you view life as an experience, your failures are just part of that experience.

What makes a performance different than an experience? It's all in your head.

Are you trying to look good? Do you want to impress others or win something? Are you looking for acceptance, approval, accolades, wild and thunderous applause? Is it painful when you don't get those things? You're probably performing.

If you're experiencing, on the other hand, you're exploring what something feels like. You are trying to see what would happen if. . . . When you're experiencing, you can appreciate negative outcomes as well as positive ones. Sure, acceptance and approval and accolades feel good, but those things don't determine success. Success is based on whether you fully immerse yourself in the experience, no matter how it turns out, and whether you learn from it. That kind of success can always be achieved regardless of how others respond.

When you're performing, your success is disturbingly short lived. As soon as you've achieved one milestone or received a particular standing ovation, the performance is over and no longer rewarding. Your unending question is, What's next?

When you're experiencing though, it's not about the end result, it's about the moment. You're not *pursuing* a feeling *after* the action, you're *having* a feeling *during* it. You can't be manipulated by a fickle, outside measure because you're motivated by a stable internal one.

So how can we let go of performance in favor of experience? Here's something that's helped me—several times a day, I'll complete this sentence: "This is what it feels like to . . ."

This is what it feels like to receive praise. This is what it feels like to be in love. This is what it feels like to be stuck writing a proposal. This is what it feels like to present to the CEO. This is what it feels like to be embarrassed. This is what it feels like to be appreciated.

Saying that, and feeling whatever comes up, instantly drops me into experience. Performance loses its primacy, and my mind releases its focus on outcome. There are no bad feelings; they all make life richer.

On the day of our wedding, I took Sue Anne's advice. And when I think back now (it's been more than fifteen years), the moments I remember most clearly and with the most fondness are the things we did not rehearse, the things that went wrong but somehow gave the wedding its life. Even our rehearsal, which clearly did not go as planned with its missing rabbi, was perfect since it led us to integrate a minister—especially meaningful for Eleanor and her family—in a more substantial way than we had anticipated.

As a performance, I have no idea how to judge it. But as an experience, it was perfect.

> Next time you find yourself in the spotlight, let go of the idea that you're "performing." Instead, allow yourself to experience the moment, and your performance will immediately go up.

● ● ● ●

# 12 "I Have No Time to Think"

## Invest in *Un*focused Focus

ON A RECENT HECTIC BUSINESS TRIP TO FLORENCE, I LUCKED OUT; my client booked me into the Four Seasons. The hotel consists of two restored Renaissance palaces, separated by eleven acres of garden. I was thrilled.

That is, until I arrived and saw that my room was in the more distant building. Every time I entered the hotel, I had to walk the length of the garden to my room. My days were jam packed with consulting, and I still had all my other work to take care of. That long, forced walk was going to steal valuable time in my day, time I could scarcely afford.

At first, I entered the garden annoyed and walked through with speed and determination. But to my surprise, each time I walked through the garden, I walked a little more slowly. Eventually, that garden walk became a transformative experience. As I meandered along the winding paths, my mind began to wander too, making connections, drawing insights, and developing ideas.

In our fast-paced, productivity-focused lives and workplaces, we are losing our gardens—literally and figuratively. We need to reclaim them.

I had lunch recently with Rajip, the chief technology officer of a large investment bank. When we returned to his office after spending an hour together, he had received 138 new e-mail messages. As we talked, the e-mail dings kept ringing out. "How can I possibly keep up?" he asked me. He can't. Rajip has close to ten thousand employees in his group. "I have no time to think," he complained to me.

*I have no time to think.* Possibly the six scariest words uttered by a leader. But they don't scare us anymore because they are so commonplace. We don't need ten thousand employees to feel too busy to think. Almost all of us feel the same way.

It's not that we're unproductive; we're astoundingly productive. We produce deliverables. We make decisions. We create and spend budgets. We direct our teams. We write proposals. Actually, in some ways, our productivity is the problem. Something's lost in an environment of manic productivity: learning.

These busy days, we rarely analyze our experiences thoughtfully, contemplate the views of others carefully, or evaluate how the outcomes of our decisions should affect our future choices. Those things take time. They require us to slow down. And who has the time for that? So we reflect less and limit our growth.

Often, it's only when our lives are forcibly disrupted that we slow down long enough to learn. An illness, a job loss, the death of a loved one—they all compel us to stop and think and evaluate things. But those are unwelcome disruptions, and hopefully, they don't occur often.

Wouldn't it be great if we could learn continuously without forced disruptions? If we could disrupt ourselves for a few moments every day in order to think and learn?

What we need is a few minutes to walk in a metaphorical garden.

My suggestion to Rajip? Think about where you do your best thinking and make it a habit to go there daily. I have made it a practice to take a variety of "garden walks" daily.

One garden walk is outdoor exercise. If I go for a bike ride, a run, or a walk, it's practically inevitable that I'll figure something out and come back with a better perspective. This is my favorite, most dependable garden for creative ideas.

Another is writing. As I write, my ideas develop and my experiences gently nudge me toward my continuously developing worldview. There's no need to share the writing—a private journal works well—and it doesn't have to take more than a few minutes.

Conversations with friends and colleagues reliably provide me with a refreshing and instructive walk in the garden. These conversations depend on the generosity of those around me, and I'm careful not to abuse that. I usually start the conversation with some version of: "Do you have a few minutes to think about something with me?" I don't let it turn into a gripe session, and I keep it focused on questioning my view, rather than seeking confirmation of it.

Garden walks can be very quick; you just have to periodically prioritize thinking over tinkering. I set my watch to beep hourly, and when it does, I ask myself how the last hour went and what I plan to do over the next hour. One minute is almost no time, but it's enough of a pause to be useful. I also take a few minutes every afternoon before leaving the office to evaluate what I experienced that day.

Chris Fox, profiled by *Fast Company* in 2011 as one of the 100 Most Creative People in Business,[7] manages all the engineers and designers working on Facebook. Like Rajip, he doesn't have the luxury of lots of time to think. "My commute is my most productive creative time," he said, "I'm not focusing on anything but I still have the energy of intense focus."

Unfocused focus. Sounds like a nice walk in a garden.

> Too busy to think, analyze, or reflect on your most important issues? Put the screens away, shut out the distracting noise, and create time every day for unfocused focus time.

● ● ● ●

# 13  Why I Returned My iPad

## Embrace Boredom

**A LITTLE MORE THAN A WEEK AFTER BUYING AN IPAD, I RETURNED IT** to Apple. The problem wasn't the iPad exactly, though it has some flaws. The problem was me.

I like technology, but I'm not an early adopter. I waited for the second-generation iPod, the second-generation iPhone, and the second-generation MacBook Air. But the iPad was different. So sleek. So cool. So transformational. And, I figured, since it's so similar to the iPhone, most of the kinks would already be worked out, so at 4 P.M. on the day the iPad was released, for the first time in my life, I waited in line for two hours to make a purchase.

I set up my iPad in the store because I wanted to make sure I could start using it the very moment I bought it. And use it I did. I carried it with me everywhere; it's so small and thin and light, why not bring it along?

I did my e-mail on it, of course. But I also wrote articles using Pages. I watched episodes of *Weeds* on Netflix. I checked the news, the weather, and the traffic reports. And of course, I proudly showed it to, well, anyone who indicated the least bit of interest.

It didn't take long for me to encounter the dark side of this revolutionary device: it's too good. It's too easy. Too accessible. Both too fast and too long lasting. Certainly there are some kinks, but nothing monumental. For the most part, it does everything I could want, which, as it turns out, is a problem.

Sure I might *want* to watch an episode of *Weeds* before going to sleep. But should I? It really is hard to stop after just one episode. And two hours later, I'm entertained and tired, but am I really better off? Or would it have been better to get seven hours of sleep instead of five?

The brilliance of the iPad is that it's the anytime-anywhere computer: on the subway, in the hall waiting for the elevator, in a car on the way to the airport. Any free moment becomes a potential iPad moment. The iPhone can do roughly the same thing, but not exactly. Who wants to watch a movie in bed on an iPhone?

So why is this a problem? It sounds like I was super-productive. Every extra minute, I was either producing or consuming.

But something—more than just sleep, though that's critical too—is lost in the busyness. Something too valuable to lose: boredom.

Being bored is a precious thing, a state of mind we should pursue. Once boredom sets in, our minds begin to wander, looking for something exciting, something interesting, to land on. And that's where creativity arises.

My best ideas come to me when I am *un*productive. When I'm running or showering or sitting, or doing nothing, or waiting for someone. When I am lying in bed as my mind wanders before falling to sleep. These "wasted" moments, moments not filled with anything in particular, are vital. They are the moments in which we, often unconsciously, organize our minds, make sense of our lives, and connect the dots. They're the moments in which we talk to ourselves. And listen.

To lose those moments, to replace them with tasks and efficiency, is a mistake. What's worse is that we don't just lose them. We actively throw them away.

"That's not a problem with the iPad," my brother Anthony—who I feel compelled to mention produced a movie called *Our Idiot Brother*—pointed out. "It's a problem with you. Just don't use it as much."

Guilty as charged. It is a problem with me. I can't *not* use it if it's there. And, unfortunately, it's always there. So I returned it. Problem solved.

But it did teach me something about the value of boredom. And I'm far more conscious now of using those extra moments, the in-between time, the walking and riding and waiting time, to let my mind wander.

Around the same time I returned my iPad, I noticed that my daughter, Isabelle, who was eight years old at the time, was unbelievably busy from the moment she got home from school to the moment she went to bed. Bathing, reading, playing guitar, eating dinner, doing homework, she was busy nonstop until I rushed her off to bed. Once in bed, she would try to talk to me, but worried about how little sleep she was getting, I would shush her, urging her to go to sleep.

We have a new ritual now, and it really has become my favorite part of the day. I put her to bed fifteen minutes earlier than before. She crawls into bed, and instead of shushing her, I lie next to her and we just talk. She talks about things that happened that day, things she's worried about, things she's curious about or thinking about. I listen and ask her questions. We laugh together. And our minds just wander.

Fight the urge to fill every empty moment in your day, especially if you need to be extra-productive or creative for a task. Our best ideas typically come to us when we are being unproductive.

• • • •

# 14 Dorit's First-Grade Classroom

## Ignore the Inner Critic

"WHO CAN TELL ME WHAT HOLIDAY IS COMING UP NEXT WEEK?" Dorit looked around the room at the circle of six-year-olds, almost all of whom raised, or rather waved, their hands eagerly.

I was with my daughter in her first-grade classroom at her Jewish day school, and I was mesmerized.

Dorit called on a little boy, who said "Purim." He was off by about a month.

"You're right that Purim is coming up soon." She smiled at the boy who smiled back. "But it's not next week. Who else?" She scanned again, this time calling on a girl.

"Tu Bishvat," the girl said.

"Very good." Dorit smiled again. "And who can tell me what Tu Bishvat celebrates?"

Now the children could hardly contain their enthusiasm. One child blurted out that it was the birthday of the trees, but he hadn't raised his hand, and Dorit took no notice as she continued to scan the hands until she called on another little boy who repeated that it was the birthday of the trees.

"Yes, that's right," Dorit said and then continued asking questions for several more minutes. While their energy never waned, nobody spoke again without being called on. When she was done, everyone sang together as they cleaned up the room to prepare for the next activity.

It felt so good to be in that classroom, I didn't want to leave. Eventually though, when it was clearly time to go, I left with a smile on my face that remained long after I had gone.

Sitting in that classroom was a lesson in people management; the positive way Dorit interacted with the children is a great model for how managers should interact with employees.

But, for me, the morning was more profound than a lesson in managing other people. It was a lesson in managing myself.

As I left the classroom I found myself thinking about whether I treat myself the way Dorit treated her students. Am I encouraging? Do I catch myself doing things right as often as doing things wrong? And when I do something wrong, do I simply move on or do I dwell on it, haranguing myself?

In other words, what kind of classroom is in your head?

We've all heard the notion that we're our own harshest critic. But shouldn't we treat ourselves with at least the same respect shown by a first-grade teacher toward her students? Why don't we?

Possibly, it's because we grow up in an academic setting that emphasizes critique over admiration. Perhaps it feels arrogant— unseemly even—to speak to ourselves with the effusive praise and positivity that Dorit spoke to her class. It might even feel dangerous to go easy on ourselves. If we did, maybe we wouldn't accomplish anything at all. Maybe we'd devolve into laziness.

But laziness is not what I saw in that classroom. Those children couldn't have been more motivated to get the right answer. They tried hard. When they got the right answer, they felt good about themselves. When they got a wrong answer, they didn't linger in shame; they simply moved on to the next question (which, as it happens, is probably the number-one behavior that leads to success over time). And they were happy.

In fact, it's the critic inside our heads—the one we think keeps us motivated—that actually demotivates us. Admonishing ourselves for doing something poorly simply makes us want to never try again. Our confidence plummets as we take seriously the voice that says we're not good enough. We become hesitant to take risks, to try new things, to experiment. And when we fail, we're less likely to try again. Our instinct to be harsh with ourselves isn't just painful; it's counter-productive.

In other words, it's not simply nice to treat ourselves nicely, it's strategic. But it's not always easy to be kind to ourselves. Certainly, Dorit has to put up with a lot of screaming kids, bad attitudes, and poor behavior. What is her secret?

Watching Dorit engage with the children—and talking with her afterward—it became obvious that what she did with the children was a lagging indicator of how she felt about them. I sensed it immediately. Clearly, the children did too. That feeling?

Love.

Think about it: when you love someone, you don't dwell on their mistakes, you move past them. If they don't know something, you don't make a big deal about it; you find the answer somewhere else. And when they succeed, you feel great about congratulating them. You encourage them when they're struggling; you try to catch them doing things right; and maybe, if you have the nerve, you sing with them as you go about your day.

Isn't that the classroom you want living in your head? Does the way you talk to yourself reflect your love for yourself? Or does it reflect annoyance, impatience, and frustration?

When we feel loved, appreciated and cared for, we try harder, take more risks, work more collaboratively, and perform better. Self-compassion doesn't make you lazy; it makes you astonishingly productive. When you feel good about yourself, you set your sights high, knowing that, even through failure, you'll be okay. That's the confidence you need to take smart chances and get big things done.

Just about all the time we spend in self-criticism is wasted, unproductive time. It's the praise that gets us going. Sure it would be ideal if the people around us treated us with love and respect. But before asking that of others, I think it's important to ask it of ourselves.

The question is how? As one particularly business-focused friend of mine asked me, "How do you operationalize love?" It's surprisingly easier than you might think.

Start by noticing your voice in your head. What do you hear when you catch yourself thinking about yourself? Do you sound like Dorit? Or do you sound like that manager you once had that you still hate? Just paying attention will begin to change the way you speak to yourself, which, in turn, will change the way you feel about yourself.

Act the way Dorit did with the children: don't reward negative behavior with attention by lingering on your failures. Instead, distract yourself by immediately getting busy doing something else.

When you succeed, on the other hand, is a great time to pay attention. Spend a minute congratulating yourself. Let your good work reflect on you. Think about what you did that led to success so you have a better chance of repeating it. Laugh with yourself. Enjoy yourself. Notice how cool you are.

At first, it might feel awkward, but feelings follow actions— once you get the hang of it, you'll gain more confidence in yourself. You'll start to take more pleasure in yourself. And if you're not there already, you might just fall in love with yourself.

At that point, what you find won't look like arrogance. Arrogance is thinking you're better than everyone else, which is often a protective mechanism born from insecurity when you don't feel good about yourself. When you love yourself, you won't need to feel better than anyone else, you'll simply feel good about yourself.

Loving yourself won't just influence the way you talk to yourself. Over time, it will influence the way you talk to the people around you, which will positively impact your colleagues, your department, your organization, and everyone who comes into contact with your organization. It turns out that speaking lovingly to yourself doesn't just make you productive, it makes everyone you touch more productive too.

In other words, if you stick with it, this little mental exercise will expand beyond just your head, and the whole world will start to feel—and act—like Dorit's first-grade classroom.

> Effectiveness begins with confidence. Next time your inner critic makes an appearance, replace it with a voice of love, care, and support; the voice you would use with a six-year-old.

• • • •

# 15   Carlos's Double Whammy

## Reclaim Your Sweet Spot

**SPENDING TIME ON PROJECTS THAT HE CONSIDERED UNIMPORTANT** was driving Carlos insane.

Carlos is an excellent leader. He's turned around every business that he's led, and the people who work for him are loyal, and under his guidance, they have quickly become powerful leaders themselves. He's exceptionally good at what he does, which is why wasting his time is so frustrating to him.

It's not that his success is based on being efficient. He's actually not particularly efficient. His success is a result of Carlos's ability to target his efforts.

Carlos is unusually adept at opportunity spotting. He notices and relentlessly pursues unique opportunities that give his firm a big win or a strategic edge. Spending time outside his particular talent threatens to create a double whammy for Carlos.

Whammy one is about what he is doing: he's spending time on things he's not good at.

Whammy two is about what he's not doing: searching for the unique opportunity for a big win or a strategic edge. Those opportunities don't come often and may be missed. Carlos feels lucky to have an insight when he does. If he's distracted, he fears the insight will pass him by.

I work with many CEOs as well as members of their leadership teams, and my experience is that Carlos is not an exception; he's the norm. Most leaders—in fact, most people who are highly successful—succeed because of a very narrow but important and unusual set of skills. We may be good at many things but we are truly great at only a small few. Becoming CEO doesn't change that.

That's why Carlos—like many of us—has a heightened sensitivity, almost a desperate fear, of being sucked into activities outside his strengths. We all should. Otherwise we will be drawn into mediocrity, where we don't do ourselves—or our organizations—any good.

But the threat to Carlos is deeper than that. People who are great at something often don't know exactly where their greatness comes from. They have a sense that it's bigger than they are. And with that sense comes a fear that the magic is ephemeral and that if they distract themselves, it will disappear. That fear is legitimate.

But here's the thing: even though we fear being distracted from our sweet spot, and even though it's tremendously counterproductive, most of us still spend the majority of our time outside it. Over forty-two thousand people have taken a distraction quiz at www.peterbregman.com and 73 percent agree or strongly agree that they don't spend enough time at work in their sweet spot, doing work they're really good at and enjoy the most. That's a massive waste of time and talent.

You have gifts that make you exceptional. If you're distracted—even if it's your boss who is asking you to be distracted—you, and she, will regret it.

So how can you avoid being distracted? Two ways:

## 1. Recognize what it is that makes you exceptional.

Time management isn't primarily about using minutes well, it's about using yourself well. And using yourself well means spending most of your time in your sweet spot, which is at the intersection of your strengths, weaknesses, differences, and passions. Carlos is ahead of the game; he already knows where he's exceptional. Whether you admit it publicly or not, you probably do too. Yet surprisingly, our knee-jerk reaction is to shy away from our sweet spots. Emphasizing our strengths feels too arrogant, exposing our weaknesses feels too vulnerable, standing out from the crowd feels too precarious, and focusing on our passions feels too indulgent. But shying away from your greatness doesn't help you or the people with whom you work. So, clearly identify your sweet spot and go there.

## 2. Protect your time.

Carlos needs to make sure that the majority of his time is spent making great use of his narrow and exceptional skill set and so do you. Unfortunately, as the results of the distraction quiz suggest, that's rare. Highly productive people stay focused. It may seem like senior people, because they lead large swaths of an organization, need to excel at a broad array of functions and disciplines. But that's not the case. Generally, their success is tied to doing a very narrow range of things very well and for the most successful, exceptionally well.

When Carlos asked me for advice, I told him to do everything he could to extract himself from those projects that drew him away from his sweet spot.

"Seeing the opportunities that will bring a big win or a strategic edge is your signature," I reminded Carlos. "It's what makes you such a valuable asset to your business. The projects that draw you away from that may or may not be a waste of time in general but, clearly, they are a waste of your time."

> If you find yourself spending a lot of time doing work you are not good at and don't enjoy, pause and refocus your energies on your sweet spot. Spend your energy where you can make the highest and best use of you.

● ● ● ●

# 16 House Rock Rapid

## Imagine the Worst

SEVERAL HOURS INTO THE FIRST DAY OF OUR PADDLE DOWN THE Grand Canyon, we came to our first significant rapid of the trip, House Rock Rapid. We got out of our boats—we were fifteen kayakers and three support rafts—and scouted the rapid from the right bank of the river.

So far, I hadn't been feeling myself on this trip. The water was bigger than anything I had paddled before, and now even small rapids—waves I could normally surf for fun—were rattling me. I felt uneasy, stiff, awkward, and scared.

I volunteered to go first, mostly to get it over with. While the other kayakers watched from land, I entered my kayak. My hands were shaking, and it took me a few tries to seal my spray skirt around the cockpit.

Adrenaline coursed throughout my body as I slowly inched my way toward the rapid. I positioned myself carefully as I entered the white water. About thirty feet upstream from the big wave, I started to paddle hard, taking short strokes to power through it. Twenty feet. Ten feet.

Bam!

A wall of water that stood at least twice my height crashed, flattening me against the back of the boat. The size of the wave startled me; it was much bigger than it appeared from land.

The wave hit with such immense force that my boat flipped, not sideways, but end over end. I was instantaneously upside down, underwater. Before I could even think about doing an Eskimo roll, the current yanked me out of the cockpit and dragged me deep down. I didn't even get a chance to take a good breath before going under. I tried to swim to the surface, but I wasn't sure which way was up.

Finally, about fifteen feet downstream, the river spit me out. I gasped for air as a large bearded river guide reached for my life jacket and tugged me onto his raft.

"Welcome to the Canyon." He laughed. I did my best to smile back as I lay on the floor of the raft, trying to catch my breath.

My pummeling was unexpected. But what happened next even more so.

When I got back into my kayak, I thought I'd be even more nervous, more hesitant, and even stiffer than before. But it was the exact opposite. I was loose, comfortable, relaxed. I did a few Eskimo rolls for the fun of it. No adrenaline. No shaking. It was a dramatic shift. My fear and uncertainty were gone. I felt refreshed.

I felt the relief of failure.

Before I was clobbered by that wave, I was terrified of being clobbered by a wave. After the clobbering, I was no longer afraid. Once I failed—and not just a misstep, but a grand, dramatic failure—I knew I could handle the other failures the river might throw at me. In fact, I didn't just *know* I could handle them, I *felt* I could.

We often hear about visualizing success, imagining yourself

in a situation saying all the right things and making all the right moves. That tactic has its place. But I want to suggest an alternative.

Try visualizing failure.

If you have a difficult conversation you need to initiate, close your eyes and imagine it going horribly wrong. Visualize yourself saying the wrong thing. In your mind, see the other person responding callously. Watch the whole thing blow up. Don't just think about it; try to feel it. Experience the adrenaline flow. Notice your heart beating. Sense the disappointment.

Okay. Now, open your eyes and realize that you've been through the worst of it. Chances are, the conversation won't go as badly as you've just imagined. And if it does, you've just experienced what you'll feel like, and you know what? You survived. It's only uphill from here.

That's what makes visualizing failure so helpful for perfectionists who often have a hard time starting things. If the failure we've just visualized is as bad as it can get, then why not try? It lowers the bar and takes the power of failure away.

It also allows you to have a conversation with your fear of failure. Mermer Blakeslee explores this beautifully in her book *A Conversation with Fear.* You can't get rid of fear, and you wouldn't want to. But engaging with your fear helps you to see it for what it really is, which is rarely as bad as you imagine.

There's another dynamic that happens when you visualize failure: you instinctively teach yourself what *not* to do, what not to say, how to recover if it goes badly, how to handle yourself in the worst case without losing control.

Here's the irony: when you visualize failure, you're actually visualizing success. You're watching yourself navigate, survive, and move through failure. Failure isn't just an annoying step on the way to success; it's as much a part of life as success. Best to get used to it.

After getting slammed by that wave, my feeling of confidence lasted the rest of the trip. Even when we got to the hardest rapid in the canyon—Lava Falls—I went through it with ease. So much so that I pulled my boat up the bank and ran it again. This second time, a wave hit me sideways and I flipped, losing my paddle.

But I had visualized that happening, and it didn't frighten me. I stayed in my boat and reached up with my hands to the surface of the water and flipped myself back over—a hands roll in the biggest water the canyon had to offer.

> Visualizing success can backfire, leaving you pressured and unprepared. It may seem counterintuitive, but visualizing failure as a way to calm your nerves and keep you on your toes will help you stay loose and be ready for challenges ahead.

• • • •

# 17 Turn the Boat Toward the Wind

## Be Prepared with a Process, Not a Solution

WHEN MY FRIEND SAM INVITED HIS NEW GIRLFRIEND, ROBYN, TO JOIN him for a sailing trip, he was relatively new to the sport. He had pretty strong skills but not a lot of experience. She had neither.

They were expecting it to be a long sail—about seven hours—and spent several days preparing. They assembled maps and prepared their route. They planned to stay close to the coast in case they needed to pull in, though there were a few short crossings where they would be unprotected. They shopped for food, packed emergency supplies, and made sure others knew their intended route.

On the day of the sail, the weather was overcast, but they decided to go anyway. Several hours into the trip—as fate would have it, right in the middle of one of their crossings—the wind picked up, and dark clouds blew in. Directly in their path, less than a mile away, was a thunderstorm. They were exposed, with lightning crackling around them.

But Sam is a levelheaded guy. And what he did—smack in the middle of the action, when most of us would panic—was astounding: he stopped the boat.

He aimed the bow of the boat toward the wind so the sails would go slack. Then he turned to face Robyn and began to discuss options. They could try to go back. They could try to go around the storm. They could try to wait it out. Or they could try to run through it.

The conversation didn't take long because they didn't have a lot of time. They weighed the options and the risks and decided to run through it. The waves were big and Robyn got seasick, but they made it through fine.

After the trip, we all had dinner, and I asked Robyn whether she wanted to go sailing again.

"Tomorrow," she responded. I commented that she must really like Sam.

"I do," she said, smiling. "But it's not *just* that. We prepared. We knew we might encounter a thunderstorm or any number of other things."

"And you knew how you would handle them?" I asked.

"No—the opposite actually. We knew that there were too many variables to have a plan for all of them. We knew we would need to make decisions on the fly."

What they needed—and what they had—was a plan for how to handle the things they didn't know how to handle, for how to be smart, in the moment, without being cocky.

"I think the best thing Sam did," she continued, "was not pretend he knew what he was doing. I love him for that. He didn't posture. He didn't rush into anything. And he didn't push me into anything. But he didn't freeze, either. We paused, we talked, and even though we were in a scary situation with imperfect information, we made a thoughtful decision fast."

That's as good a description of powerful leadership—and powerful living—in the twenty-first century as I can imagine.

We live and lead in a world of imperfect information, guaranteed surprises, and unpredictable occurrences. Storms, both real and metaphorical, are waiting to happen. Our instinct is to try to predict their arrival, but doing so is futile. Trying to eradicate their risks is fantasy. And even though we may have planned meticulously, believing that we're prepared for whatever the future will bring is folly. The most effective people are able to navigate ambiguity.

But if we can't possibly know what will happen tomorrow, how can we be prepared? One way to do this, as I wrote about in the previous chapter, is to visualize failure to help stay calm and be ready for anything. Another way is to prepare to be unprepared.

In the face of the unexpected:

## 1. Stop the boat.

If momentum is driving you to make a decision quickly, don't give in. As Sam did in front of the thunderstorm, turn the bow toward the wind and let the sail go slack. If you're in a meeting, take a bathroom break. In your office, get up and take a walk. In other words, do what we so rarely give ourselves an opportunity to do: pause and think. Paul Petzoldt, legendary mountaineer, environmentalist, and founder of the National Outdoor Leadership School, used to say that the first thing you should do in an emergency situation—once you know it's safe—is smoke a cigarette. Proverbially, anyway.

## 2. Assess your actual options.

Don't waste time wishing things were different or trying to force-fit your previous plan to the new, unforeseen situation. Start with a blank slate: think about the outcome you want given the new situation, the information you have at hand, and the resources available. Then lay out your options.

### 3. Sail.

Based on your new assessment, make a decision, and commit. Even if the decision isn't ideal, even if it's not giving you everything you hoped for originally, accept that it's the best under the circumstances and move forward without hesitation.

No matter how much preparation we do, navigating our way through a new economy, a new competitive landscape, or a new team will constantly put us in situations for which we are unprepared. Becoming comfortable acting in the face of the unanticipated is a huge asset.

After that day, Sam and Robyn continued to sail together, and their relationship grew. One day, they went out on Sam's boat and, in a calm expanse of open sea, Sam got on one knee and, unexpectedly, asked Robyn to marry him. Robyn paused, but not for too long, and then, relying on all her newfound handle-the-unexpected sailing experience, knowing there would be a life of surprise awaiting her, she said yes.

> Ditch the habit to plan for every future scenario. Instead, become comfortable navigating ambiguity and respond to the unexpected by taking a breath, making decisions based on the best information you have at the time, and committing to them.

· · · ·

PART TWO

# Strengthen Your Relationships

· · · ·

In part 1, I shared how pausing for even four seconds is all you need to reset your mental habits—from how you can get the most from yourself to succeed, to how to best react in stressful situations. Now, the challenge is to use that power to connect more productively and profoundly with others. Four seconds certainly helped me deal with Sophia, my seven-year-old who had barged in to tell me she and her brother Daniel had flooded the kitchen. I was about to yell at them, but I paused and took a breath.

During that few-second pause, I looked at Sophia's face. And at that moment, Daniel, my five-year-old, ran in, and I looked at his face too. What I saw in their faces was fear. It was immediately clear to me that they knew what had happened was bad. Really bad.

Yes, I was angry. Yes, I wanted to yell. But I paused long enough to ask myself what was needed in this situation. Would yelling help? Looking at their faces, I knew the answer. My kids already knew something was very wrong. They didn't need me to reinforce the point by screaming. That would only create further stress in a situation that was already filled with stress.

That's the power of four seconds.

In the previous chapters, we explored the value of slowing down and resisting the impulses and temptations to act in ways that, when looked under the microscope, don't serve our interests. I discussed pausing for a few seconds to overcome our self-defeating mental habits and to replace them with smarter choices.

And we explored ditching behaviors that leave us frazzled, over-whelmed, and spent, and embracing ones that help us act from our strength and connect with ourselves deeply.

In the chapters that follow, we'll explore how to best connect with others. Often people either connect deeply to themselves—and lose sight of other people—or they connect deeply to other people and lose themselves. But true power comes from doing both at the same time. Staying connected to yourself and from that place, connecting deeply with others brings productive outcomes as well as happiness.

The problem is that, while we often long to connect with others, our tendencies leave us disconnected. In difficult or stressful situations, we follow our knee-jerk reactions to get de-fensive, argue, or blame others. We end up alienating ourselves and others.

In part 2, we'll focus on replacing the bad habits that keep us away from forging strong relationships, with good habits that help us connect deeply and peacefully with others.

Back at my apartment, while the temptation was almost over-whelming, I did not yell at Sophia and Daniel, nor did I blame them, nor even ask them what happened. It was instantly clear to me that none of that would have helped.

"Okay, quick," I said as I closed my laptop and got up, "What do we need to do?"

"Shut the water off!" Sophia screamed. It turns out that there was so much water in the kitchen, they were afraid to wade through it to turn off the tap.

So, together, we went into action mode. We ran into the kitchen, and I picked up Daniel, holding him above the water so he could turn off the tap himself. Then we got every towel in the house and a couple of blankets and mopped it all up. We moved fast, but instead of crying and screaming, we ended up laughing as we worked.

In part 2, I'll show you how to strengthen your relationships by subverting the knee-jerk reactions that separate you from others and by honing new habits and behaviors that create deeper, more meaningful connections. I will also show you how to listen so people feel heard, how to speak so people listen, and how to navigate difficult conversations and situations with poise and confidence. You will learn:

- why, contrary to popular business wisdom, you actually *are* here to make friends;

- why arguing never resolves conflict—it only solidifies opinions;

- why a pep talk is the worst thing you can offer a person who has experienced failure;

- why taking blame is a smarter move than blaming others; and

- why listening for what is unsaid is often more helpful than listening to what is said.

As you read the chapters in this section, you will be on your way to connecting with others more deeply and constructively.

# 18 A Lesson from My Mother-in-Law

## Prioritize Relationships

SUSAN HARRISON, MY MOTHER-IN-LAW, DIED AFTER A LONG AND courageous battle with cancer. Like most of us, she was not famous. If you didn't know her, you probably didn't know of her. She lived in the relatively small community of Savannah, Georgia.

Yet she did some amazing things there: she was the first ordained woman deacon in Georgia; she founded a soup kitchen; and she helped create the Savannah Homeless Authority. In addition, she raised three children, and some would add, a husband.

One of the problems we faced after her death was finding a church big enough to hold the people who wanted to attend her funeral. We picked the largest one we could find, with seating for six hundred, and still many had to stand in the back and along the aisles.

Susan had a particular quality that drew people in. It wasn't her accomplishments. It wasn't money. She had no access to famous or important people. She couldn't hire you; she wasn't a stepping-stone.

Susan was, quite simply, a really good friend.

Being a good friend is an art. You have to give of yourself, but not so much that you lose yourself. You need to know what you want and pursue it while helping others achieve what they want. You need to have personality while making room for, and supporting, other people's personalities. You need to care about, and even love, people you might disagree with (I'm pretty sure she didn't vote for the same candidates as her husband). You need to be willing to give at least as much, if not more, than you take.

When it comes to forging deep friendships in our competitive work spheres, our instinct is often to keep people at arm's length. If you watch even a single episode of any reality TV show based on a competition—*The Apprentice, Survivor, Top Chef, America's Next Top Model, The Bachelor, The Amazing Race* (it doesn't matter which)—you'll hear a single phrase come up more often than any other:

"I'm not here to make friends!"

Apparently many of the contestants believe that in order to win they can't worry about how they affect others. As one contestant on *The Apprentice* so eloquently said, "It's nothing personal. This is f——g business."

Even if we don't believe that being cutthroat is better than being collaborative, many of us simply don't make time for building the kind of strong and supportive friendships that characterized Susan's life. We're too involved in our own lives, too busy with our own challenges, and too focused on being productive in our own work to really focus on others.

But is this the smartest, most productive way to move through life?

According to the research, giving to others—a reliable way of fostering friendships—makes us happier than taking things for ourselves. According to research led by Dr. Elizabeth Dunn at the University of British Columbia, money can buy happiness—as long as you spend it on other people.[8]

Researchers conducted three studies. First, they surveyed more than six hundred Americans and found that spending money on gifts and charities led to greater happiness than spending money on oneself.

Then they looked at workers who had just received bonuses and found that their happiness was not based on the size of their bonus but on the decision they made about what to do with whatever amount of money they received. Those who spent more of their bonus on others were happier than those who spent the money on themselves.

Finally, the researchers simply gave money to a number of people, instructing some to spend the money on themselves and others to spend the money on others. At the end of the day, the ones who spent money on others were happier.

So having friends and treating them generously is clearly a winning strategy in life. But do we need friends in business?

Well, let's look at the data. If you're looking for a job, you'd better have friends. The number-one way people find new jobs is referrals by friends.

Once you're on the job, having a best friend at work is a strong predictor of success. People might define "best" loosely (think of this as kindergarten where you can have more than one "best" friend), but according to a Gallup Organization study of more than five million workers over thirty-five, 56 percent of the people who said they have a best friend at work are engaged, productive, and successful while only 8 percent of the ones who don't are.[9]

Another remarkable study,[10] spanning decades, revealed that friendships in high school were a strong predictor of increased wages in adulthood—to the tune of 2 percent per person who considered you a close friend. In other words, if in high school three people listed you as one of their closest same-sex friends, your earnings in adulthood would be 6 percent higher.

Want to stay in that job you have? Then you'd better have friends. As a friend of mine who runs sales for a successful technology company told me recently, "People try hard not to fire their friends. It's the difference between 'He's a good guy,' and 'I don't know about that guy.'"

During Susan's last few days she was surrounded at all hours by her family and friends. During those moments, she managed to get some advice out. Among her parting words? "Surround yourself with a loving community."

In other words, it's a pretty good bet that we really are here to make friends.

> The drive to be productive often leads us to de-prioritize our friendships, but developing strong relationships with others is one of the keys to unlocking our sustainable success.

• • • •

# 19 The Hardest Part Is After the Speech

## Show People Who You Truly Are

I OFTEN FEEL AWKWARD WHEN I GO TO A CONFERENCE. RELUCTANT to sidle up to a stranger and introduce myself, I roam, like I did at college parties, self-conscious, seltzer water in hand, not fitting in. In the midst of a sea of people chatting away enthusiastically, I am uncomfortable and alone.

But when my plane from New York landed in Austin, Texas, for South By Southwest (SXSW), the music, film, and interactive conference, I was excited. I was speaking on a panel, and since everyone told me SXSW is a blast, I had given myself an extra day to explore the conference.

But it didn't play out like I had hoped. I arrived just in time for my panel, then I did a book signing, and then, well, then I was at a conference. I went to a conference party and just stood there, shy, embarrassed, and reluctant to reach out and meet people.

I was annoyed with myself. What's my deal?

I was about to leave when I thought, instead of judging myself, why not take this as an opportunity to explore an uncomfortable emotion? So I stood there and felt what awkward felt like.

It felt awkward.

But, soon, I recognized something deeper behind my shyness, something more pernicious. Once I finished the panel, I had no role and no purpose. I realized that when I'm not accomplishing something, I'm not sure who I am. I was having a conference-generated identity crisis!

My sense of self is dangerously close to my sense of role. I'm a writer, a speaker, a consultant, a father, a husband, a skier, and so on. But who am I when I'm not actively being those things? Who am I without my accomplishments—past, present, or future?

Just me. Which, it turns out, was unsettling.

I don't think I'm alone. It's why, within a minute of meeting someone, we begin to define ourselves by our roles, our status, and our relationships to others. We think it's because other people need that information to know us, but standing alone at that party, I realized I'd been fooling myself. Other people don't need that information to know me. I need that information to know myself.

Once I understood the source of my discomfort, I resisted the urge to drop a name or tell people I had just given a talk or written a book or something else to identify a solid role for myself that would make me look and feel good.

Instead, I paid attention to what it felt like to be without any identity other than my presence. I noticed my desire to be noticed and my feelings of insecurity. But I also noticed my feelings of strength and trust in my observations and in myself. I began to relax, and once I did, I didn't feel nearly as insecure.

Then something funny happened. People started to approach me.

Out of the blue, a woman walked over and introduced herself to me, and we started talking. Then she waved a colleague over. They didn't know me and weren't looking for anything from me, nor I from them. We were just three people connecting. As soon as we parted, a man came over. Again, I introduced myself by name but not by role. Again, we had a great conversation and a nice, human connection.

I didn't tell people that I'm a writer or that I run a consulting company or any other role-defining facts. I just met them as Peter. And they met me as themselves. It took some getting used to, especially at a conference where we tend to define ourselves by our roles and where people talk to each other while looking around to see if there's someone more useful to talk to.

But it's a mistake to launch into your business plan when you meet someone new—even at a conference where the point is to peddle your business plan. People invest in you first, then your plan. So show them you first, then your plan.

That's precisely why shedding our roles—at least initially— even at a conference and even if there is something we want from others, is such a good idea. People will trust you if you trust yourself. And to trust yourself you have to step out from behind the curtain. You have to expose yourself, and you have to be willing to be vulnerable. When you allow people to see you—as impressive and vulnerable as you are—then they will trust you because they will know you.

So how, at a conference when you don't know anyone, can you engage in a conversation without identifying your role? It's not easy. You'll be fighting against the tide. Try asking open-ended questions, and try getting personal. Eventually you'll find out more about your fellow conference-goers, and they'll find out more about you.

A conference—life, for that matter—is just a bunch of human beings bumping into other human beings. Most of whom feel awkward about it. Most of whom, more than anything, would love to be seen for who they are, not just the roles they represent. We can give that to each other.

It might be awkward at first, but I think it's our best shot at having a meaningful experience in a situation that often leaves us feeling shallow. Being known for who we are, not just what we are, is clearly good for us, and it might just be good for business too.

> When you meet someone, let go of the impulse to define yourself by your role or title, or to come across in any particular way. Instead, take the risk to simply be yourself and notice how much connection that creates.

• • • •

# 20 He Broke Up with Her in a Text

## Don't Let the Package Distract You from the Message

**ELEANOR AND I CAME HOME FROM DINNER ONE NIGHT, AND FOUND** our babysitter, Leslie, in tears.

"Is everything okay with the kids?" I asked.

"Yes. They've been sleeping the whole time. It's not that."

"Do you want to talk about whatever it is?" I asked her.

"He broke up with me in a text message." she said, holding her phone. She had been dating Ned for a few weeks and they had grown close quickly. The breakup text was a complete surprise to her.

"A text?" I said. I had never met Ned, but I was already angry at him for such a cruel move.

"He broke up with you?" Eleanor asked, wanting to learn more.

As soon as I heard Eleanor, I realized my mistake; a mistake many of us make when we communicate about anything sensitive, which includes just about everything.

We confuse the package with the message. We get so distracted by the awkward, sometimes inappropriate *way* in which someone is communicating that we miss what the person is communicating.

It's not just the mode of communication. Sometimes it might be a tone of voice—a yell, a sarcastic remark, or a particular set of words that are used. A simple question like "How did you come to that conclusion?" could be taken as a challenge, an accusation, a support, a query of curiosity, or something else.

With Ned's breakup text message, I was focused on the *package*—how uncool it is to break up with someone in a text message. (By the way, just for the record, I think it *is* uncool to break up with someone in a text message). But Eleanor looked beyond that. She was focused on the message itself—what Ned was trying to say in his text.

People's tendency to focus on the package rather than the message plagues us and decimates our productivity. For example, my friend Malcolm, was only a few months into a new job, when he confessed that he was afraid to write e-mails to his new colleagues:

"It seems like everything is politics," Malcolm told me. Then he mimicked some of his colleagues: "Why did you CC that person? Why didn't you CC me? Why did you bring up that budget issue?" He paused and looked into space as he mused, "I spend half my time trying to craft my communications just right. What a waste! Frankly, it's easier and smarter to just not communicate."

Here's the real issue: we are all clumsy communicators—both in what we say and in what we hear. Add to that cultural, religious, geographic, gender, age, language, and socioeconomic diversity, and it's a miracle we understand each other at all. Our natural shortcomings as communicators are precisely why we spend so much of our time confused, upset, disappointed, suspicious, or angry at many of the people around us.

The solution? Try this:

*Notice.* Anytime you feel a negative emotion about something said or written to you, it's a warning sign that you might be getting distracted by the package. If you feel anger, sadness, frustration, disgust, and disbelief, you'll know it's time to move to step 2.

*Pause.* Take a deep breath. Then recognize you're vulnerable to reacting emotionally to *how* something was communicated, and remind yourself that communication is hard and often done poorly. Cut yourself, and everyone else, some slack. Don't assume malicious intent. Don't take it personally. Resist the urge to be offended.

*Interpret.* Now reread what was written, or think about what was said, and unscramble it. Think about what the person was *trying* to convey. Search for value. Strive for understanding.

*Respond.* A good rule of thumb is to use a different medium than elicited your emotional response. If a text upset you, don't text back. If an e-mail set you off, pick up the phone. And when you do reply, ignore the package and focus on the message.

As a general rule, assume clumsiness. Picture someone who is moving fast, trying to get a lot done—someone who's not skilled at communicating perfectly. Assume they're not a jerk. Overlook their inelegance. Then, when it's your turn to speak, address the real issue not the clumsiness.

As soon as I realized I had gotten distracted by Ned's use of a text message, I switched gears, took Eleanor's lead, and asked Leslie to read us Ned's text. As we unpacked the actual message—as we read between the lines—it became clear that Ned was overwhelmed by his feelings. He needed to slow down. But it was also clear that he really liked Leslie.

After the three of us discussed it, Leslie decided to ignore that Ned had used a text message and call him to talk about what he was experiencing. Ned's text message turned out to be a present. A present Leslie almost discarded because the wrapping was so ugly.

But she took the time to unwrap it and it led to their conversation. Then to a walk. Then to dinner. And then . . . well, that's a package only time will unwrap.

> As we keep up with the speed-of-light pace of our busy lives, we've all become clumsy communicators. Don't get distracted or offended by how the message is communicated or delivered. Assume the best, look beyond how someone communicates with you, and respond to what's really going on.

• • • •

# 21 I Want to Be Like You When I'm Seventy-Seven

## Choose to Be Inspired by People

I WAS LIFTING WEIGHTS AT MY GYM, A COMMUNITY CENTER IN NEW York City, when he caught my attention.

His name, I later found out, was Marvin Moster. He stood a few inches over five feet, mostly bald with some white hair on the sides of his head, sporting a mustache, and wearing a light-blue shirt and dark-blue shorts. In the obvious ways, he was unremarkable. And yet, I couldn't help noticing him.

He was older—I guessed in his seventies—and he was boxing with a trainer, punching in a rhythm they had obviously practiced before, ducking his head whenever the trainer threw a hook. Two things struck me: he was in excellent shape—evidenced by his balance, his rhythm, and how vigorously he was punching—and he was having fun.

"How old are you?" I asked him when he took a break.

"Seventy-seven," he told me with a smile.

"I want to be like you when I'm seventy-seven," I said.

His smile broadened. "And I want to be like you now."

His laugh was infectious. It made me feel good just being around his energy, soaking in his enthusiasm. At least in that moment, he seemed delighted to be himself. That's when the thought occurred to me.

"Can I take your picture?" I asked him.

"Sure," he said, "What for?"

I pulled out my camera phone as he posed with his boxing gloves raised.

"I want you on my fridge," I told him.

I don't know Marvin. I don't know whether he's healthy or sick, wealthy or poor, happily married, unhappily married, single, divorced, or widowed. I don't know his politics or what his friendships are like or whether he's gay or straight or what he does besides go to the gym. I don't even know if he's a nice person.

But I do know that I wanted a little bit of what I perceived in Marvin—his energy, what appeared to be his sunny outlook—in me. So I took his picture. Which got me thinking, "Why not start a collection of pictures of ordinary people, about whom I know very little, but who inspire me with some quality I want to nurture in myself?"

Like the bus driver in Paris who, after I asked him which stop to get off for my hotel, asked me for the exact address and then pulled out his iPhone at a red light to check the map and suggest the closest stop.

Or the taxi driver who declined to take me to the airport because she was finishing her shift but pulled over, got out of her cab, and waited with me to make sure I got another taxi before leaving.

These are ordinary people in ordinary situations who surprised and inspired me. I want that to rub off on me.

But wait a second. I've written about high-profile leaders in this book. People like the late Dr. Allan Rosenfield, the public-health trailblazer whose work saved the lives of millions of people in developing countries. Shouldn't he be on my fridge instead of a moderately helpful bus driver?

Maybe. But being reminded about the bus driver can change my behavior today. I can look at his picture and be a little more helpful to others. He reminds me of something simple I want to nurture in myself. Same with Marvin.

I am not saying these people should inspire everyone—that everyone should put a picture of Marvin on their fridge. I'm not suggesting we build a leadership model based on their examples. I am suggesting you keep your eye out for your own Marvin. And when you find him or her, you take a picture.

This idea may seem simplistic. People are complex. If I really knew any of these people, I might not want them on my fridge. I don't know why Marvin is boxing; maybe he spent four years in prison for some heinous crime and wants to stay in shape because he's planning another one? Most likely, I'm just projecting characteristics I like onto other people. I can't honestly say that the inspiration isn't more about me than it is about them.

But here's the thing: we're always projecting things onto other people. We just often choose to be critical more readily than we choose to be inspired—to project more negative things onto people than positive.

In fact, we seem to rarely miss an opportunity to be disappointed. We focus on what people are doing wrong, on their weaknesses and shortcomings. We gossip and complain. We get frustrated and passive-aggressive. We find ourselves constantly surprised by the flaws of our colleagues: how could he/she/they do that?

What if, instead—or at least in addition to not missing an opportunity to see the flaws in others—we chose not to miss an opportunity to be inspired? If we gossiped about things people did that energized us without fixating on the things that disappointed us? If we looked for sparks that ignited our enthusiasm and induced our goodwill? And if we allowed those sparks to light our fires of passion?

If nothing else, we'd feel better about the people around us, the world we live in, and ourselves, if only for a moment. And maybe, after a few weeks or months, we'd end up with refrigerator doors filled with reminders of people who inspire us—not for lives thoroughly well lived—that's probably too high a bar—but for drops of inspiration.

Every time I look at that picture of Marvin, it makes me smile. And it encourages me to eat a little better and exercise a little more.

So, who's on your fridge?

> Don't give in to your instinct to find flaws in others; choose instead to find something about them that impresses you. Find inspiration in the simple things they do.

• • • •

# 23 A Lesson from My Mother

## Refuse to Write Someone Off

**WHAT DO YOU DO WHEN YOU HAVE A COMMUNICATION IMPASSE WITH** someone you care about?

Jim is a friend and colleague who I hadn't seen for a year. It's been a hard year for Jim, and I called him frequently as he navigated his business through tough times. When I last saw him, Jim asked me to meet with a client of his, Ed, for a few minutes as a favor. I agreed. But when I arrived at Ed's office a few days later, the receptionist told me he was out of the country. He had been expecting me a day earlier, she said, and was disappointed when I hadn't shown up. I apologized and left.

I immediately called Jim, who checked his e-mail and discovered that he had given Ed the wrong day. I told him I was embarrassed and asked him to send a handwritten note to the client apologizing and explaining the error. He promised he would.

We hadn't talked about the missed meeting since it happened. Jim's troubled business had been the focus of our conversations. But I was speaking at a conference in a week, and I expected Ed to be there; I wanted to know how things had resolved. When I saw Jim at a party, I asked him whether he had written the letter.

He got angry and snapped at me. "I didn't write the letter. Peter, I'm broke. I haven't had a minute to do anything. Can't you understand that?"

I was taken aback, hurt. I mumbled something and walked away. But I couldn't get it out of my head. Why was he snapping at me?

I've always believed that if I simply talk things through with someone I can resolve any issue, so I walked back to him.

"Jim," I said, "I know it's been a hard year, but why are you lashing out at me? I asked about the letter because I might see Ed at a conference. The letter isn't such a big deal to me, but your response really bothers me."

"Well," he answered, "I'm sorry my response bothers you."

*Sorry my response bothers you.* He didn't apologize for asking me for a favor and then putting me in an embarrassing situation. He didn't apologize for not writing the letter. He didn't even apologize for his response. All he did was acknowledge that his response bothered me—which bothered me even more.

Intellectually, I understand what was going on. Having a business crash is highly emotional, very strained, and extremely difficult. In that light, my question about the letter seemed trivial and out of place. Add to that his own shame about not having followed through on his commitment and the result was misplaced anger toward me. I get it. But emotionally it felt like a betrayal of all I had done to support him over the past year. And it left me wondering: now what?

I could try to talk with him about it again, but I was pretty sure it would go the same way, and I would leave feeling more hurt.

I could go around talking to other people about him, getting their perspective, complaining. But that's not who I want to be.

I could write him off completely. But we travel in the same circles, and it's unlikely we could avoid each other. I didn't want to get that rush of negative adrenaline every time we were in the same room. And anyway, do I really want to write off everyone whose actions hurt me? I'm sensitive; I might end up alone. Finally, and perhaps most important, I really like Jim. He's been a good friend for twenty years, and I enjoy his company. He's funny, interesting, and often warm. I don't want the friendship to end.

The rest of the party was awkward, and I left with a bad feeling, not knowing what to do. Eventually, I called my smartest advisor.

My mother is surrounded by people who love her. Recently she told me she was going out with someone who had betrayed her; he went behind her back to buy a rare item that had been promised to her. The seller maintained his commitment to my mother, and my mother maintained her relationship with both the seller and the betrayer. How was she able to get over it?

"I know what to expect from him," she told me of her betrayer. "That's the kind of person he is."

"Did you ever talk to him about it?" I asked her.

"No," she said, "Why should I? It wouldn't make a difference. I'm not going to change him. And talking about it won't change the situation."

"But how can you still spend time with him? Don't you get angry when you see him?"

"I'm too tired to be angry every time someone does something I don't like. And I don't want to be alienated from everyone. I enjoy him for his other attributes. But I know what to expect from him."

My mother's insight is profound. Her advice?

Live with it.

Jim's response isn't about me, it's about Jim, and I'm living in the space between never speaking to him again and trying to fix things by speaking to him. That space is called accepting people as they are.

Jim's response informs me about Jim. He has a reputation for snapping at people and for using anger to intimidate and avoid. It's just that he never directed it toward me before. It's a part of his character. He may change, but I'm not counting on it. My interaction with him offered me data. Data that tells me more about what I should expect from Jim in the future.

But snapping at me isn't all I should expect from him. And by knowing what to expect, I can appreciate the parts of Jim I like without becoming distracted by the parts I don't; I can accept him fully for who he is, without illusion; and I can keep myself safe in our relationship when he acts in ways I don't like.

In retrospect, I would still ask Jim if he had written the letter, but when he snapped at me, I would have said, "I know this year has been hard for you, and I'm sorry you've had to go through that. I understand you didn't write the note. That's good to know in case I see Ed at the conference next week." And leave it at that. No hurt. No anger. No avoidance. No passive-aggressive comeback—just acceptance of the situation and of Jim.

Will my relationship with Jim be more superficial from now on? At first, I was sure it would be, but I'm going to try hard not to let it be. People are imperfect. That includes my mother's betrayer, it includes Jim, and it also includes me. That's why it's important not to write off Jim. If I did, then I'd end up writing myself off too. Accepting Jim's limitations enables me to accept my own.

This includes accepting the fact that there are some situations I can't resolve with *more* communication.

> Resist the impulse to write off someone who has hurt or disappointed you. Most of the time, they aren't betraying you; they're just being their imperfect selves, struggling with their own issues. Accept the person and their limitations, and move on.

● ● ● ●

# 23 The Inescapable Parking Ticket

## Walk Away from an Argument

IT WAS LUNCHTIME, AND THE SEVEN OF US—TWO KIDS AND FIVE adults—would be in the car for the next three hours as we drove from New York City to upstate Connecticut for the weekend. We decided to get some takeout at a place on the corner of Eighty-Eighth and Broadway. I pulled along the curb and ran in to get everyone's orders.

In no time, Isabelle, my then eight-year-old, came running in the restaurant.

"Daddy! Come quick! The police are giving you a ticket!"

I ran outside.

"Wait, don't write the ticket; I'll move it right away," I offered.

"Too late," she said.

"Come on! I was in there for three minutes. Give me a break."

"You're parked in front of a bus stop." She motioned halfway down the block.

"All the way down there?" I protested.

She said nothing.

"You can't be serious!" I flapped my arms.

"Once I start writing the ticket, I can't stop." She handed me the ticket.

"But you didn't even ask us to move! Why didn't you ask us to move?" I continued to argue as she walked away.

And that's when it hit me: arguing is a waste of my time. Not just in that situation with that police officer. I'm talking about arguing with anyone, anywhere, anytime. It's a guaranteed losing move.

Think about it. You and someone have an opposing view and you argue. You pretend to listen to what she's saying, but what you're really doing is thinking about the weakness in her argument so you can disprove it. Or perhaps, if she's debunked a previous point, you're thinking of new counterarguments. Or maybe, you've made it personal: it's not just her argument that's the problem. It's her and everyone who agrees with her.

In some rare cases, you might think the other person's argument has merit. What then? Do you change your mind? Probably not. Instead, you make a mental note that you need to investigate the issue more to uncover the right argument to prove the person wrong.

When I think back to just about every argument I've ever participated in—political arguments, religious arguments, arguments with Eleanor or with my children or my parents or my employees, arguments about the news or about a business idea or about an article or a way of doing something—in the end, each person leaves the argument feeling, in many cases more strongly than before, that he or she was right to begin with.

How likely is it that you will change your position in the middle of fighting for it? Or accept someone else's perspective when they're trying to hit you over the head with it?

Arguing achieves a predictable outcome: it solidifies each person's stance, which, of course, is the exact opposite of what you're trying to achieve with the argument in the first place. It also wastes time and deteriorates relationships.

There's only one solution: stop arguing. And resist the temptation to start an argument in the first place.

If someone tries to draw you into an argument? Don't take the bait. Change the subject or politely let the person know you don't want to engage in a discussion about it.

And if you're in the middle of an argument and realize it's going nowhere? Then you have no choice but to pull out your surprise weapon. The strongest possible defense, guaranteed to overcome any argument: listening.

Simply acknowledge the other person and what she's saying without any intention of refuting her position. If you're interested, you can ask questions—not to prove her wrong—but to better understand her.

Listening has the opposite effect of arguing. Arguing closes people down. Listening slows them down. And then it opens them up. When people feel heard, they relax. They feel generous. And they become more interested in hearing you. And that's when you have a shot of doing the impossible: changing that person's mind—and maybe your own—because listening, not arguing, is the best way to shift a perspective.

Then, when you want to leave the conversation, say something like, "Thanks for that perspective" or "I'll have to think about that," and walk away or change the subject.

I'm not saying you should let someone bully you. This weekend I was in a long line and someone cut in front of me. I told him it wasn't okay, and he started yelling, telling me—and the people around me—that he had been there all along, which was clearly not true. I began to argue with him, which, of course, proved useless and only escalated the fight.

Eventually, a woman in the line simply drew a boundary. She said, "No, it's not okay to simply walk in here when the rest of us are waiting," and she stepped forward and ignored the bully. We all followed her lead and, eventually, he went to the back of the line. Arguments: 0. Boundaries: 1.

When I went online to pay the parking fine, I tried to dispute the ticket. Before arguing my case though, a screen popped up offering me a deal: pay the penalty with a 25 percent discount, or argue and if I lose, pay the entire fine. I thought I had a good case, so I argued and a few weeks later, lost the case.

Next time, I'm taking the deal.

> Next time you find yourself at the brink of an argument, walk away—you'll never win it. If you're stuck in one, change tactics and listen: it's your only chance to change the other person's mind.

● ● ● ●

# 24 Don't Blame the Dog

## Take the Blame Instead

I WAS AT A PARTY IN GREENWICH VILLAGE IN NEW YORK CITY. IT WAS crowded, with about twice as many people as the space comfortably fit. There was a dog in the mix too. But it was a casual event, and we all spent a lot of time in the kitchen, cooking and cleaning.

I was at the sink washing dishes when I heard the dog yelp behind me. I turned just in time to see a woman curse at the dog as it dashed out of the kitchen. She had obviously just stepped on his foot or tail.

"Watch out!" she shouted after the dog, then saw me looking at her and added, "He's always in the way."

Really? You step on a dog, and then you blame the dog? Who does that?

Actually, a lot of us do.

We start blaming others at an early age, usually to escape parental anger and punishment, but also to preserve our own self-esteem and self-image. Then the behavior sticks, often well into our adulthood. I—and I am sure you—see people in organizations point fingers all the time.

Sometimes it's at a departmental level: a struggling sales group blames a poor product, while the product people blame an ineffectual sales team or maybe lax manufacturing. Blaming a department or a product feels safer than blaming a person since it appears less personal, can pass as an attempt at organizational improvement, and might seem less defensive. But it's counter-productive, as the transparency of culpability betrays its disguises.

A few years ago, I sat at a table with the leaders of a major stock exchange. They were struggling with setting goals for the year. The CEO, to whom they all reported, was not in the room. I asked them what was getting in the way. "We need direction from senior leadership," they answered in agreement.

"Seriously?" I was stunned. "Look around," I said, raising my voice a little, "Everyone in the organization is looking for direction from you! You are senior leadership."

"No," the head of something answered with the others nodding in agreement, "The CEO isn't here."

I retorted, "You're blaming the CEO? You're waiting for him to tell you what to do? At your level? Really?"

An awkward silence followed. Then we got to work turning the company around.

Blaming others is a poor strategy and not simply because everyone can see through it. Or because it's dishonest. Or because it destroys relationships. Or even because while trying to preserve our self-esteem, it actually weakens it. There's a more essential reason why blame is a bad idea: blame prevents learning.

If something isn't your fault, then there's no reason for you to do anything differently.

However, when something is your fault and you don't admit it, in all probability, you'll make the same mistake in the future, which will lead to more blame. It's a cycle that almost always ends badly.

Recently, a CEO I work with fired Bill, one of his portfolio managers. He didn't fire him for poor results. He fired him for blaming his poor investment results on everything except himself. The CEO was only looking for one thing from Bill: awareness of the mistakes he was making. But Bill continued to deny his role in his poorly performing portfolio.

The CEO was right to fire him. If Bill couldn't admit to the mistakes he was making, why wouldn't he make the same mistake tomorrow? Would you trust Bill with your money?

Thankfully there's a simple alternative to blaming others: Take the blame for anything you're even remotely responsible for.

This solution transforms all the negative consequences of blaming others into positive ones. It solidifies relationships, improves your credibility, makes you and others happy, reinforces transparency, improves self-esteem, increases learning, and solves problems. It's as close as I've ever seen to a panacea.

Once you've taken responsibility for something, you can do something about it. It takes courage to own your blame, and that shows strength. It immediately silences anyone who might try to blame you—what's the point if you've already taken the blame? The "blame you" conversation is over. Now you can focus on solving problems.

Being defensive makes you slippery. Taking responsibility makes you trustworthy. You might think it puts you at risk because others may see an opening and jump on you, but that's not what usually happens.

I was running a strategy off-site at a high technology company with a CEO and his direct reports. We were looking at some problematic numbers from the previous quarter. One by one, each leader was trying to argue that he or she was not, ultimately, responsible for the issues, pointing to the other areas that contributed. Then Dave, the head of sales spoke up. He proceeded to list the mistakes he felt he personally made and what he wanted to do differently in the future.

His colleagues didn't pile on. In fact, they did the opposite. They began to say things to dilute his blame. One by one, they started taking responsibility for their role in the challenges the company was facing.

Taking the blame serves as an example. When you take the blame, others get embarrassed about not taking the blame themselves. When they see you don't get shot, they feel emboldened to take the risk.

And even if they don't assume responsibility for their role in the situation, you will now be able to avoid making the mistakes you've made in the past, which, ultimately, is the key to your success. By taking the blame, Dave changed the course of that meeting, and as it turns out, the course of the company. He also got promoted.

There is one tricky thing about taking the blame. To take the blame, you need to have confidence in yourself and your capability. You need the personal strength to accept failure. You need enough self-esteem to believe you can learn from your mistakes and succeed another day. You need to accept failure as part of life and not a final sentence on who you are as a person.

In other words, it's okay to step on a dog. It happens. Just don't blame the dog.

> Contrary to our natural urge to defend ourselves and excuse our mistakes, taking the blame is the power move, strengthening your position, not weakening it.

• • • •

# 25 Hardware Stores Don't Sell Milk

## Learn Other People's Rules of Engagement

A FEW MONTHS AGO, ELEANOR CAME HOME UPSET AFTER AN INCIdent with Michelle, one of the parents at our daughter's school. That afternoon, when Eleanor said hello to Michelle, Michelle completely ignored her. Thinking maybe Michelle hadn't heard her, Eleanor said hello again, this time louder. Again, no response.

Michelle wasn't speaking on the phone or in a conversation with another parent. In other words, Michelle wasn't *unable* to respond, she just *refused* to. Eleanor was getting the silent treatment. Not one to give up, Eleanor said hello a third time. Finally, Michelle mumbled something without looking up and walked away.

Eleanor wasn't friends with Michelle. They had only spoken a few times in the past, most notably when she called Eleanor to complain about something our daughter did. Still, Eleanor was thrown off balance by Michelle's cold shoulder. It was one of those small things that's hard to get out of your mind. She wasn't *expecting* it.

We are constantly shocked by the things other people say and do or by the things they don't say and don't do. How can my boss have ignored me? How can my colleague have taken the credit? How can my employee have made that mistake? Can you *believe* my manager said that to me in front of all those other people? How can my partner be so inconsiderate? Why doesn't my spouse appreciate what I do for her?

When I coach executives or mediate conflicts between leaders, each person is always amazed at how the other people behave. This has led me to a very simple conclusion: the problem is not us, and it's not them. The problem is our expectations.

It's not that people behave well or badly. It's that we *expect* them to behave *differently* than they do—even when they have proven our expectations wrong time and time again. Should you still be surprised when your boss for the one hundredth time doesn't invite you to a meeting? Or when you send a colleague a nice e-mail and it goes unanswered—again?

Here's my advice: don't go to a hardware store and get upset when they won't sell you milk. In this case, the answer to frustration is acceptance. It's amazing how changing your expectations can change your experience.

Because the world is more global and organizations are more diverse, the likelihood we will interact with people very different from us is increasing exponentially. And people who are different from us do things we don't expect or want them to do. Sometimes they don't look at us when we speak to them. Sometimes they talk back. Sometimes they don't talk at all. They defy our expectations, and we feel frustrated.

Remember the golden rule? Treat other people the way *you'd* like to be treated? Forget it. It doesn't apply anymore, if it ever did. Try this new rule instead: treat other people the way *they'd* like to be treated.

If you don't like to be micromanaged, for example, you probably try to avoid micromanaging others. But there are some times and some places where that would be a mistake, like India, for example.

According to Michael S. Schell, coauthor of the excellent book, *Managing Across Cultures: The Seven Keys to Doing Business with a Global Mindset,* Indian workers prefer—and expect—to be micromanaged. Mike told me recently, "That ultimate sin of Western managers is the best way to get things accomplished in some cultures. Once you begin to treat people the way they want to be treated, you'll find the results much more rewarding. When operating in a new country, we don't just need *word* translators. We need *people* translators."

In some cultures, it's important for meetings to start on time. In others, it makes no difference. In some cultures it's rude to interrupt. In others, it's simply the norm. Understanding other people's expectations can help you reset your own. And that helps you work with them more effectively.

When I'm sitting in a meeting with Yukiko, my Japanese partner, and she doesn't speak, I might assume she agrees with what I'm saying. But I'd be wrong. It's not that she *agrees* with me, it's just that she *would never disagree with me in public.* If I understand that, I won't be surprised when she doesn't follow through.

Still it's almost easier to understand Yukiko because I'm from New York and she's from Tokyo. I expect her to be different. But

Chris in the office next door, who's also from New York? That's a different story. I shouldn't need instructions on what to expect from him.

But I do because each one of us is, in effect, from a different culture. We have different parents, different teachers, different experiences, different hopes and dreams, and different successes and failures. Even if we understand the same words, we're still speaking different languages.

So instead of getting frustrated with other people, learn their rules of engagement. If you pretend each person is from a foreign country you don't fully understand, you'll be more open to accepting him or her.

Then, when someone defies your expectations, don't get mad. Just change your expectations to more accurately align with reality. Once you understand other people's operating instructions, you might decide to approach them differently, use different words, or be more or less aggressive.

Or you might decide to leave—to go and work somewhere else with other people or join another community group or find new friends. Because once you accept others, once you realize you simply can't buy milk at a hardware store, you might decide you don't want to be in a hardware store at all. I'm not saying people can't change. I'm just saying you're setting yourself up if you expect them to.

"Do you think I should call Michelle to talk with her about this afternoon?" Eleanor asked me, still stewing over getting the cold shoulder.

"That depends," I answered, "will you be okay with it when she blows you off?"

Instead of getting frustrated with people when they don't meet your expectations of how they ought to behave, adjust your expectations to more accurately reflect the behavior they regularly engage in. Learn how that individual operates and adjust your approach accordingly.

• • • •

# 26   Sophia's First Powder Day

## Meet People
## Where They Are

ELEANOR AND I WERE FAST ASLEEP AT MY PARENTS' HOUSE IN
upstate New York when my daughter, Sophia, who was five years
old at the time, came running in.

"Look out the window!" she screamed, as she pulled on our
shades. I looked at my watch: 6 A.M. Sophia was jumping with
excitement as the shade opened, revealing about a foot of new
powder.

"Let's go skiing!"

A few hours later, I stood with Sophia and sister, Isabelle, who
is three years older than Sophia, at the top of an intermediate
slope we had all skied many times. But this time was different.
Northeastern powder is not the light, fluffy stuff of the West. It's
heavy and hard to ski, especially when you weigh forty-five
pounds.

Isabelle struggled but managed to navigate the new conditions. Sophia, on the other hand, fell almost immediately. She
laughed, got up, and started again. A few feet down the slope,
she fell once more. Again, laughing, she got up. Now Isabelle
started laughing too.

But not me. I was worried. This was too much for Sophia. She might get hurt, and her ski class started in fifteen minutes. At this rate, she would never make it.

I shouted a few words of encouragement and advice. But her laughter was making it hard for her to ski. Was she falling on purpose because it was fun?

I stayed behind her so I could help when she fell, but I was becoming increasingly frustrated. I yelled at her to stop playing around. But she kept falling and laughing.

I looked at the time. "Sophia!" I shouted. "Come on, stop fooling around. It's not funny. We're going to miss class."

"I'm trying," she yelled back.

I paused for a moment, looked up, and took a deep breath. The beauty of the snow-covered trees was incredible. And that's when I finally realized I'm an idiot.

Here was my awesome five-year-old having an outdoor experience I want to encourage. And even though it was hard and scary and challenging, she was handling it gracefully, having the time of her life. And how did I help? By yelling at her.

It seems obvious now. But at the time my response felt perfectly natural. Which is the point, actually. It felt natural because it reflected how *I* was feeling: fearful, frustrated, and worried about getting Sophia and Isabelle to their lesson without injury and on time.

My mistake? I forgot that the situation wasn't about me. I forgot to focus on the needs of my audience, in this case a five-year-old skiing powder for the first time. That's presentation and communication skills 101. I would never make the same mistake if I were giving a speech or working with a client. In other words, if I were *thinking*.

In the heat of the moment, it's easy to skip the thinking part. An employee comes to us with substandard work, and we get angry. But is that really going to help the employee do better work next time? If the reason for the poor performance was that the employee didn't care, and my anger frightened him into caring more, then maybe. But poor performance is rarely caused by lack of fear. It's usually because of a misunderstanding or lack of capability—in which case, asking questions would almost certainly be more helpful.

That's hard to do because when we're angry, we respond with anger. And when we're frustrated, we respond with frustration. It makes perfect sense. It's just that it doesn't work and it won't help.

The solution is simple: When you have a strong reaction to something, take a deep breath and ask yourself a single question: What's going on for the other person? Then, based on your answer, ask yourself one more question: What can I do or say that will help *them*?

In other words, don't start from where *you* are, start from where *they* are. What do they need in that moment? Some advice? A story about what you did in a similar situation? Perhaps just an empathetic ear? Or maybe simply some patience.

Imagine your favorite employee—the one you spent all that time developing—told you she was thinking of leaving your team for another job offer. You might feel angry and betrayed, but would it help to get angry at her? No, you'd be better off asking questions about what's working and what's not.

Once I realized my mistake, I got angry at myself for almost stomping out Sophia's enthusiasm. But I didn't beat myself up for long. I took a few deep breaths and just watched her. She skied a few feet, fell, laughed, got up, and started skiing again.

Watching her laughing at her mistakes reminded me not to take myself so seriously. It turns out that meeting people where they are doesn't just help them. Sometimes it helps you too.

> In the heat of a frustrating situation, don't respond based on how you feel in the moment—anger, annoyance, irritation—but rather based on what the other person needs to resolve the situation.

• • • •

# 27 It Was a Long Shot

## Become a Great Receiver

**EVEN BEFORE I RELEASED THE DISC, I KNEW IT WAS A LONG SHOT.**
And unfortunately, it was a clumsy one too.

We were playing Ultimate Frisbee, a game similar to U.S. football, and we were tied 14–14 with a time cap. The next point would win the game. I watched the disc fly over the heads of both teams. Everyone but me ran down the field. I cringed, helplessly, as the disc wobbled and listed left. Still, I had hope it could go our way.

My friend Sam was on my team.

Sam broke free from the other runners and bolted to the end zone, but the disc was too far ahead of him. He would never make it. At the very last moment, he leapt. Completely horizontal, Sam moved through the air, his arms outstretched. Time slowed as he closed in on the disc. The field was silent as he slid across the end zone, shrouded in a cloud of dust. A second later he rose, Frisbee in hand. Our team erupted in a cheer.

Sam's catch won us the tournament.

It also taught me a great lesson: never underestimate the value of a talented receiver.

I was reminded of Sam's catch recently after broaching a sensitive topic with Alba, a client. The conversation was about some concerns I had about an upcoming meeting she was leading as well as my own insecurity about how I could help. Before I spoke with her, I was hesitant and worried. Was I overstepping my bounds? Was I exposing myself? Would she reject my thoughts? Would she reject me?

I entered the conversation awkwardly, apologizing, and offering too much context. Even once I broached the issue, I felt tentative, unclear. I cringed as I felt my words hang in the air.

Thankfully, though, Alba turned out to be a Sam-level receiver.

Alba listened without a trace of annoyance. She asked questions—not to defend herself or refute my thoughts—but to understand my perspective more clearly. She was gracious, skilled, and accepting. Her ability to receive me, and my opinions, led to a deep and valuable conversation about her performance, my role, and the needs of her team. A few weeks later, she showed up powerfully and led a remarkable meeting.

Typically, we choose our leaders for their skill at conveying messages clearly and powerfully. But, in my experience, it's their ability to receive messages that distinguishes the best leaders from the rest.

So how do you become a great receiver?

*Be courageous.* We often attribute courage to the speaker, but what about the receiver? I may have been scared broaching topics with Alba, but I had the advantage of time and preparation. I could control what I said and how I said it. I was able to think about it beforehand, write down a few notes, and test my thoughts with someone else. The receiver has no such advantage. Like Sam, he has to receive my throw, however, whenever, and wherever it lands. He has to be willing to listen to something that might make him feel afraid or insecure or defensive. And if he is a great receiver, he will take in the information or message thoughtfully, even if the delivery is awkward or the message jarring. That takes tremendous courage.

*Don't judge.* Receiving is as much about what you don't do as it is about what you do. Resist the temptation—blatantly or subtly—to be critical of the speaker or what the speaker is saying. Don't argue with her, poke fun at her, shame her, act aggressively, turn on her, become defensive, or act cold toward her.

*Be open.* In order to receive a pass in any sport—and at work and in life—you need to be free, open, and unguarded. Yet we often guard ourselves. Powerful feelings like fear, anger, sadness, and insecurity do their best to block our ability to receive a pass. If you want to be a talented receiver, your task is to feel your feelings without letting them block or control you or your response. Breathe. Acknowledge what you're feeling to yourself— maybe even to the other person—without dwelling on it. Reiterate what you're hearing, ask questions, be curious. Not curious in an I-will-find-out-enough-information-so-I-can-prove-you-wrong way, but curious to understand what the person is saying and what's underneath what they're saying.

If you can be courageous, avoid judging, and stay open— even if the toss is awkward and the message unsettling—then, like Sam, like Alba, you'll be able to catch pretty much anything.

And when you're skilled at that, you'll be a most valuable player of any team you're on.

Next time you feel the impulse to reject feedback or someone else's opinion or idea—drop the fight and open up yourself to the other person's input. The better you are at receiving, the more likely it is that people will talk to you.

● ● ● ●

# 28 A False Start Gets You Disqualified

## Empathize First. Help Them Feel Better Later.

ELEANOR AND I WERE VISITING SOME FRIENDS ON A SATURDAY when their nine-year-old daughter, Dana, came home. She was close to tears, barely holding it together.

"Oh sweetie," her mom said. "What happened at the swim meet?"

Dana is an excellent swimmer. She trains hard, arriving at swim practice by six most mornings and swimming some afternoons as well. And her efforts are rewarded; she often wins her events, scoring points for her swim team. It is clear she is very proud of these wins.

It isn't like that for all her endeavors. She struggles with some subjects in school, doing extra math homework to keep up with the other kids and getting special help with her reading. But she always works hard.

"I was disqualified," she told us. She swam the race well but dove in a fraction of a second before the starting gun went off: a false start.

We were in the foyer of the house, and she sat down on the bottom stair of the staircase, her swim bag still on her shoulder, staring into space, almost expressionless.

"Honey," her dad said, "there are a lot more swim meets in the season. You'll have other chances to win."

I told her, "The fact that you left the block prematurely means you were at your edge. You're trying not to waste a millisecond in hesitation. That's the right instinct. You misjudged the timing but that's okay. The more you do this, the better you'll get at it."

"Every swimmer on every team has been disqualified at some point," Eleanor said. "It's part of the sport."

"I'm sure your coach will help you practice your starts before the next meet," her mom said, "and you'll figure out exactly when to spring off the block so that you don't waste a second but you don't dive too early either. You'll get it."

Nothing we said seemed to have an effect on her. Nothing changed her expressionless stare. Nothing helped.

Then her grandmother Mimi walked over.

We were all standing over Dana, when Mimi moved through us and sat down next to her. She put her arm around Dana and just sat there quietly. Eventually, Dana leaned her head on Mimi's shoulder. After a few moments of silence Mimi kissed Dana's head and said, "I know how hard you work at this, honey. It's sad to get disqualified."

At that point, Dana began to cry. Mimi continued to sit there, with her arm around Dana, for several minutes, without saying anything.

Eventually Dana looked up at Mimi, wiped her tears, and said, simply, "Thanks, Mimi." And I thought, *every leader, every manager, every team member, should see this.*

All of us except Mimi missed what Dana needed.

We tried to make her feel better by helping her see the advantage of failure, putting the defeat in context, teaching her to draw a lesson from it, and motivating her to work harder and get better so it doesn't happen again.

But she didn't need any of that. She already knew it. And if she didn't, she'd figure it out on her own. The thing she needed, the thing she couldn't give herself, the thing that Mimi reached out and gave her?

Empathy.

She needed to feel that she wasn't alone, that we all loved her and that her failure didn't change that. She needed to know we understood how she was feeling and that we had confidence that she would figure it out. That we trusted her.

I wanted every leader, manager, and team member—every person—to see that because the empathetic response to failure is not only the most compassionate, it's also the most productive.

When I sit with you in your mistake or failure without trying to change anything, I'm letting you know that you're okay, even when you don't perform. And counterintuitively, feeling okay about yourself—when you fail—makes you feel good enough to get up and try again.

Most of us miss that. Typically, when people fail, we blame them. Or teach them. Or try to make them feel better. All of which, paradoxically, makes them feel worse. It also prompts defensiveness as an act of self-preservation. (If I'm not okay after a failure, I'd better figure out how to frame this thing so it's not my failure.)

Our intentions are fine; we want the person to feel better, to learn, to avoid the mistake again. We want to protect our teams and our organizations. But the learning—the avoidance of future failures—only comes once they feel okay about themselves after failing. And that feeling comes from empathy.

Thankfully, the expression of empathy is fairly simple. When someone has made a mistake or slipped up in some way, just listen to them. Don't interrupt, don't offer advice, don't say that it will be all right. And don't be afraid of silence. Just listen. And then, after some time, reflect back what you heard them say—what you feel they're feeling. That's it.

I said simple, not easy. It's hard to just listen and reflect back. It's hard not to give advice or solve a problem. Hard, but worth the effort.

After some time, Dana got up from the stairs, we all had dinner, and then she went to watch some TV. We were talking in the living room when she came in to say good night.

"How are you feeling?" I asked her.

"Okay, I guess." She shrugged. "I'm still bummed."

I almost told her not to worry, that it would be okay, that she would feel better in the morning, that there was always the next race, that she had lots of time to practice.

Almost.

"I understand," I told her. "It's a bummer."

> Our well-meaning attempts to make people feel better almost always backfire. Try empathy instead; it communicates trust. and people feel most connected—and perform best—when they feel trusted.

• • • •

# 29 It's Not About the Shampoo

## Listen for the Unspoken

TO BE FAIR TO MYSELF, I MUST SAY I WAS PRETTY FOCUSED AT THE time, working in my office on an article. When my wife called my name, I really didn't want to be interrupted.

We were going away for the weekend and Eleanor wanted my help packing. She shouted from the bedroom, raising her voice enough to be heard between the two rooms. I yelled that I was working on deadline.

She yelled back, "Could you at least pack the shampoo?"

Now that just seemed ridiculous to me. She wanted me to get up from my computer, walk over to the bathroom, grab the shampoo bottle, and put it in our suitcase? She was in the bedroom already packing everything. It would take her ten seconds to do it herself.

"Listen," I shouted, "can't you just put the shampoo in the bag? It doesn't seem like a big deal."

"Fine!" she yelled, and as soon as I heard the tone of her voice, I knew I had made a critical error. I had missed the entire point of her request. I thought it was about packing the shampoo, but that wasn't the case.

Welcome to the land of clumsy communication, misunder-standings, and unnecessary arguments escalated by not paying enough attention.

On one level, Eleanor's request was about packing the sham-poo. But even then, I had misunderstood what she meant. She thought I hadn't yet packed my own toiletry kit and was asking if, when I did, I could pack some shampoo into a small bottle for the family: a reasonable request.

On another level, Eleanor's request had nothing to do with the shampoo; it had to do with the fact that Eleanor is always the one who packs for the family, and she was sick of it. She asked me to pack the shampoo because she needed to feel like she wasn't the only one packing. Like we were in this together. In some ways, she was being generous by asking me to do something as simple as pack the shampoo. She could have asked me to get all the children's clothes together, but she didn't. She was being sen-sitive to my deadline. I'd missed that.

And then at the deepest and most profound level—a level impossible to reach effectively in a conversation carried out be-tween two rooms—I eventually learned that Eleanor's request was about a nagging question: this, she wondered as she was packing, is how she's using her Princeton education? Her mas-ter's degree? Her role as the packer represented, to her in that moment, the failure of equality, women's rights, and her own decision making about her work and family choices.

All those things were packed densely inside her request. But I wasn't really paying attention, since I was in the middle of writ-ing. Which one of us was right? In situations such as these, it doesn't matter who's right. It only matters how we communicate, connect, and collaborate.

It's not unusual to miss the real communication going on behind the words. It's typical. We're taught to clearly and rationally express our needs, desires, requests, and expectations. And we're taught to listen carefully. But how often do we do either? And when we don't and a miscommunication follows, who's responsible for making the first move to clear up the miscommunication?

Whoever sees it first.

And that's the real challenge. It's hard to listen to what someone is saying and understand the real need hidden behind the words. How do we know when there's something deeper and more significant going on?

My clue, after being jolted by her tone, was Eleanor's words *at least*. Could I "at least" pack the shampoo? There's an edge to that. A sign that something else is going on.

So what should you do? Don't slam the other person for making no sense. Don't accuse him of being unreasonable. And don't make the mistake of telling him what he's really trying to say. All of that will backfire. Instead, even if you think you know what's going on, ask a question.

Once I thought I figured it out, I was able to go to Eleanor and, after apologizing, ask her if she was feeling all alone in preparing the family to leave for the weekend. Yes, she told me, she was. And she hates that feeling. I let her know that I understood and appreciated it. And then I got the shampoo.

When someone expresses a request, demand, assertion, or thought that doesn't seem to make sense, resist the temptation to react. Instead, pause. Ask yourself what's going on. Ask the other person. And if it's an easy thing to do, then consider just doing it. It's hard to work so closely with colleagues day in and day out. It's like a marriage. And in the case of remote workers from multiple cultures and countries, it's like a long-distance cross-cultural marriage.

Making those work is hard. It helps to cut the other person a little slack. Give him the benefit of the doubt. "Be kind," a common saying goes, "for everyone you meet is fighting a hard battle." The nice thing about that perspective, that compassion, is that it doesn't just make other people's lives easier. It makes our own easier too.

> If someone makes a request or demand or says something that doesn't seem reasonable—especially if the person is usually reasonable—resist the urge to react and give them the benefit of the doubt. Chances are there's something deeper going on that is not being said.

● ● ● ●

# 30 My Best Birthday Ever

## Give the Gift
## of Appreciation

**EVEN THOUGH IT'S A FEW YEARS BEHIND ME, I STILL REMEMBER MY** forty-third birthday.

Forty-three doesn't mark a new decade. It's not one of those birthdays people usually celebrate in a grand way, and mine was no exception. No one threw me a lavish surprise party. I had a few small dinners with close friends and family. I opened two presents.

And yet that birthday stayed with me. I remember feeling so appreciated, respected, and loved. Because on this particular not-a-big-deal birthday, in addition to those two presents, I received some other gifts—gifts that cost nothing and that I have come to realize are, actually, a very big deal.

It got me thinking, What's the point of gifts anyway?

On a basic level, we give gifts because we're supposed to give. On certain occasions—birthdays, anniversaries, dinner parties, the end of the year—it's customary. Underlying that custom is an important purpose: appreciation. We give people gifts to show them that we are grateful for them and value the role they play in our lives.

But here's a common misconception: the bigger, more valuable the gift, the more it expresses our appreciation. I know people who've received huge stock grants who feel severely underappreciated. That's because gifts don't express appreciation; people do. And when people don't express it, neither do their gifts.

The gifts I received that meant so much to me on my forty-third birthday? Eleanor asked a small group of my friends to write me a note of appreciation, "a thought or intention or poem," she wrote to each friend, "that encourages him to accept himself just as he is."

*Just as he is.* There is no more powerful way to acknowledge others than to be thankful for them just as they are.

And yet we almost never do this. Especially in a corporate setting where we often ask people to change and where we value them for what they can do for us and for the company. Think of our corporate end-of-the-year rituals: performance reviews, holiday parties, and sometimes, if we're lucky, bonuses. Performance reviews are supposed to identify our strengths, and the best reviewers spend most of their time dwelling on strengths. But it's not a review unless we also look at weaknesses, areas "to develop," places where we fall short. In other words, immediately after we tell people how great they are, we tell them how they aren't good enough.

Holiday parties usually include a speech by the CEO or other leader thanking people for their hard work over the year and encouraging them to continue working hard over the next year. It's an important ritual, but it's impersonal, given to the entire company or department at once. And it's typically about what we've been able to accomplish, not about who we are. People don't feel individually recognized.

And bonuses are a business deal, based not on appreciating us for who we are but on compensating us for what we achieved, often delivered with no ceremony and no clearly expressed appreciation. The huge stock grants that left people underappreciated? They were, literally, placed on people's empty chairs overnight. No note. No conversation. Just a piece of paper on a chair.

I'm not suggesting these rituals aren't important. People work together in organizations in order to accomplish things, so it makes sense that our organizational rituals appreciate people for accomplishing things and for increasing their ability to accomplish more things in the future.

But I'd like to suggest an additional way to appreciate the people around us. A way that costs nothing and feels great to everyone involved: in a handwritten note, tell them why you appreciate them. Not for what they do for you. Not for what they help you accomplish. Not even for what they accomplish themselves. Just for being who they are.

When I share this idea with people, I often get pushback. "If I appreciate people simply for being themselves," I'm told, "then what's their motivation to keep working hard? To keep growing?"

One executive I know won't tell someone they're doing well without also telling them he wants them to keep it up. It's a subtle but destructive habit that creates mistrust. It's like giving a gift to someone and then warning them that you might take it away if they no longer deserve it. When people feel that mistrust—or when they feel underappreciated—they work less hard. They vent about their dissatisfaction with others. They become less motivated.

That's the crazy part—we're giving the gift to show our appreciation, and if we don't do it with the right appreciation, we end up making people feel underappreciated. The people whose stock grants were simply left on their chairs didn't feel thankful; they felt angry and resentful.

It's counterintuitive, but the more someone feels appreciated without pressure to perform, the better they'll perform. Their motivation will come from an internal drive rather than an extrinsic force. It's a simple formula: if you want people to feel appreciated, appreciate them with no demands.

If you're skeptical about this approach—maybe you think it's too touchy-feely, too sappy—just think about what it would feel like to receive unadulterated, unmitigated appreciation in a note from the people around you.

So be generous with your gifts of appreciation, even with people about whom you feel conflicted. Perhaps you don't like everything about them. Maybe you don't always appreciate who they are. That's okay. This isn't a performance review. You don't have to address everything about each person. This is a gift. There's no reason to hoard your appreciation; it's unlimited in supply. Just think about what you do appreciate about people and describe that part. Let them know what about them makes you smile, what you admire, and what makes them special to you.

Then hand them your notes and thank them, individually, for working with you. Or, if you're feeling bashful, just leave the notes on their chairs overnight; there's no risk they'll open them and feel under-appreciated.

I know, for me, it made my otherwise insignificant, mid-decade birthday the most significant one yet.

Our attempts to motivate other people with gifts and rewards can actually demotivate them when these express how we value them for what they can do for us and for the company. Instead, acknowledge people by expressing what you appreciate about who they are. The more someone feels appreciated without pressure to perform, the better they'll perform.

• • • •

# 31 Getting a Free Upgrade to First Class

## Appeal to People's Generosity

MY FLIGHT FROM NEW YORK TO PARIS WAS DELAYED—MAYBE IT would be canceled—and the passengers at the gate were frustrated. Most were sitting quietly in their frustration, periodically looking up at the screen and mumbling the things that people mumble when they feel annoyed but powerless like "We're never gonna get out of here!" and "Can you believe this?"

Then there was this French couple, for whom mumbling was not sufficient. They were having difficulty communicating in English, which I knew, as did everyone else in the airport, because they were in a loud argument with the gate agent. They had that "Do you know who I am?" posture, with some "I'm not leaving until I get what I want" thrown in for good measure.

I sidled in closer to hear what the commotion was about. As I understood it, they were angry because they had tickets but no seat assignment and were afraid they would be booted off the flight. The gate agent, who I later found out was able to give them a seat assignment, refused to assign them seats. She assured them that they would be on the flight when—and if—it left, but she said she had to focus on getting the flight off the ground, and "right now, no one has a seat because the flight isn't going anywhere."

Something was lost in translation; they heard, "You don't have a seat, and you're not going anywhere." Which, of course, made them feel even more anxious and powerless. They reacted to this powerlessness by trying to exert power. They insisted even louder that they did, in fact, have seats, just not seat assignments, which is what they were asking for. And she had better give them that! To which she responded, and I'm quoting her, "No!"

It would be easy to give the gate agent advice on how to handle the situation more effectively. But it's more interesting to figure out what the French couple should do. Because if you set aside who's right in this situation, and if you set aside the language barrier, what you have left is a situation we're all in all the time: a power struggle. The gate agent clearly had the power; she could choose to give the French couple a seat assignment or not.

Sometimes this struggle is departmental: Sales wants something from Marketing, but Marketing isn't giving it to them, so Sales yells louder, maybe with a threat or two for effect. Other times, the power battle is more personal: one team member wants something from another team member and tries to use her power to get it. Sometimes, even, it works.

But more often than not, it fails. Grabbing power, especially when you don't have it, is unpredictable, feels bad to both parties, and is bullying. The collateral damage to the relationship is almost always high. There's got to be a better way to get what you want when you're powerless in a situation.

Thankfully, there is, and discovering it won me a free upgrade to first class: let go of the illusion that you have any power at all. It's getting in the way. People, when asked and respected, will often willingly do the exact thing they're refusing to do when they feel like you're pushing them.

As soon as I heard the gate agent say, "No!" I stepped in. Literally. I stepped between the French couple and the agent and interrupted their conversation. I had a secret weapon: I speak French.

I asked the gate agent to give me a moment and spoke to the couple in French, explaining what the agent was saying. Then, I turned to the gate agent and explained what the couple thought she was saying.

Once everyone had calmed down, the French couple apologized and let the gate agent know that they recognized how hard the delayed flight must be on her. They said they knew she didn't have to give them a seat assignment but explained how anxious they felt. They asked whether, in this particular situation, even though she was clearly so busy trying to get the flight off the ground, she might be willing to give them seat assignments to help them. After a short conversation, she gave them new boarding passes with seat assignments.

Sometimes, it really does help to appeal to a powerful person's generosity.

Here's what's interesting: in the business world, it often feels like everyone else always has the power. At any moment, customers can take their business elsewhere, employees can change jobs, and colleagues can pursue their own, personal agendas.

No matter what our positional power, we're better off appealing to people's generosity. Even if we're paying them, it's useful to see those around us as volunteers, which means issuing more requests than orders and creating relationships built on trust and respect rather than hierarchy and politics.

If you notice other people in a power struggle, consider stepping in the middle—not to choose sides, but to bridge the gap.

Sometimes people need a momentary disruption in their battle to see each other as people and reach into their own deep well of generosity. And usually, they're too deeply enmeshed in their argument to see beyond their own stance. The interruption by a third party can help both sides get beyond themselves.

When the gate agent thanked me for intervening, I figured I'd give it a try too. I told her I was happy to help, and followed with "I know you have so many other people you're trying to satisfy. And I don't even know if it's possible—it's probably against the rules—but if there is some way you had the ability to upgrade me, some chance of an extra seat in first class, I would be so appreciative. It would make the flight an awesome treat. If there were any way . . ."

Well, as it turned out, because of the plane equipment problems, the airline had to put us on a different plane, one with a larger first-class cabin. As I boarded the new plane, I was met by a pleasant surprise: the agent took my old boarding pass and generously handed me a new one, with a new seat assignment—in first class.

> When you are interacting with someone who has power over you, don't engage in a power struggle by issuing demands and threats. Instead, appeal to their generosity. If asked respectfully, people will often happily do the very thing they're refusing to do when they think you're trying to push them.

• • • •

# 32   Why Tim Didn't Get the Promotion

## Don't Skip Your Thank-Yous

JOHN, THE CEO OF A SALES ORGANIZATION, SENT AN E-MAIL TO TIM, an employee several levels below, to compliment him on his performance in a recent meeting. Tim did not respond to the e-mail.

About a week later, he was in John's office applying for an open position that would have been a promotion into a management role, when John asked him whether he had received the e-mail. Yes, Tim said, he had. Why, John asked, hadn't he responded? Tim said he didn't see the need.

But Tim was wrong. John's e-mail deserved, at the very least, a thank-you.

Tim didn't get the promotion. Was he passed over solely because he didn't thank John for the positive feedback? No. But was Tim's lack of response one of several reasons that convinced John he should choose a better candidate? Undoubtedly.

Before you accuse John of being trivial or oversensitive, before you condemn his poor hiring judgment, consider what saying thank you represents.

On a basic level, it communicates that you received the e-mail.

While there's a lot of advice that discourages writing thank-you e-mails because they contribute to e-mail overload, I disagree. I answer every real e-mail I receive because I want to avoid the recipient's "Did Peter get my e-mail, and what's he thinking?" angst. It takes three seconds to respond "Thanks!" and it completes the transaction initiated by the sender.

But an e-mail that contains emotional content—like a compliment—deserves something longer: a real, thought-out thank-you as opposed to a simple I-received-your-e-mail thank-you. When you offer a real thought-out thank-you to someone, you're acknowledging her effort, appreciating her thoughtfulness, recognizing her intent, and offering feedback on the impact of her actions.

Still, it's more than that. Those things are rational, but saying thank you is mostly an emotional act. It connects one person to another. Saying thank you doesn't just acknowledge someone's effort, thoughtfulness, intent, or action. It acknowledges the other person.

Acknowledging other people is a critical responsibility—perhaps the critical responsibility—of a great manager, especially in sales. Actually, great manager is too high a bar. I might say it's the critical skill of a good manager, but even that's understating the necessity and impact of acknowledging others.

Go ahead and argue: we're all too busy at work and in life to spend time exchanging pleasantries; if John needs so much stroking, he can't possibly be a good CEO. He's out of touch with the digital age where unanswered e-mails are the accepted norm; if Tim is doing his work well, that's all that matters; people are paid to do their jobs, and they don't need to be thanked; saying thank you to your CEO for a nice e-mail is nothing more than brownnosing.

I would disagree with all those arguments. It doesn't take long to say thank you, but it does take caring. John is an excellent CEO, with a staff, board, and shareholders who love him and for whom he delivers a high growth rate and excellent results. Not answering someone's communication—text or e-mail or phone call—is not an accepted norm, it represents a fundamental breakdown in communication about which I often hear people complain. Tim might be good at certain aspects of his job, but he's not "doing his work well," if he's not acknowledging the people around him. And finally, saying thank you isn't brownnosing; it's nice.

At a time when we are all too busy and have too much to do, it's tempting to focus only on essential communications. It seems unproductive to spend time saying thank you.

But the opposite is true. Our instinct not to send thank-you e-mails (whether in an effort to save us time or to avoid overloading others with unnecessary messages) actually backfires. It ends up creating more work for everyone—especially for the original sender, who wants to know whether we had received their message and invariably will e-mail again to confirm. A thank-you not only confirms receipt of their message—saving us and them time—it creates goodwill and makes relationships stronger, more resilient, and less likely to devolve into energy-sucking conflicts.

The consequences of not saying thank you become more obvious if you take away the digital element. How would you feel if you complimented someone in person and he just walked away from you without saying anything? Weird, right?

Saying thank you—sincerely and with heart—feels good. Not just to the person receiving it but also to the person offering it. And that's part of work too. It's hard to remember, as we process our hundredth e-mail, that behind each message is a person. Tim would have done well to remember that.

> While skipping sending a thank-you message might seem like a time-saving strategy, it rarely pays off. People like to have their efforts and their own messages acknowledged. Doing so creates the kind of goodwill that might make your relationship immune to future time-sucking conflicts. Saying thank you is never a waste of time.

• • • •

# 33 No

## Establish Boundaries with Others

IRENE IS A GREAT COLLEAGUE. A SENIOR MANAGER IN A LARGE CON-sulting firm, she pitches in when the workload gets heavy, covers for people when they're sick, and stays late when needed, which is often.

She's also a leader, serving on boards and raising money at charity auctions. She tries to be home for her kids at dinnertime, but she often works into the night after they've gone to sleep (i.e., on nights when she's not at a business dinner).

If you catch her in a moment of honesty, you'll find out that she doesn't feel so great. In fact, she's exhausted.

Irene can't say no. And because she can't say no, she's spending her very limited time and already taxed energy on other people's priorities, while her own priorities fall to the wayside. I have experienced the same thing myself. So, over time, I experimented with a number of ways to strengthen my no.

Here are the nine practices I shared with Irene to help her say a strategic no in order to create space in her life for a more intentional yes.

### 1. Know your no.

Identify what's important to you and acknowledge what's not. If you don't know where you want to spend your time, you won't know where you don't want to spend your time. Before you can say no with confidence, you have to be clear that you want to say no. All the other steps follow this one.

### 2. Be appreciative.

It's almost never an insult when people make requests of you. They're asking for your help because they trust you, and they believe in your capabilities to help. So thank them for thinking of you or making the request/invitation. Don't worry; this doesn't need to lead to a yes.

### 3. Say no to the request, not the person.

You're not rejecting the person, just declining his invitation. So make that clear. Let him know what you respect about him—maybe you admire the work he's doing, or recognize his passion or generosity. Maybe you would love to meet for lunch. Don't fake this—even if you don't like the person making the request, simply being polite and kind will communicate that you aren't rejecting him.

### 4. Explain why.

The particulars of your reason for saying no make very little difference, but having a reason does. Maybe you're too busy. Maybe you don't feel like what they're asking you to do plays to your strengths. Be honest about why you're saying no.

### 5. Be as resolute as they are pushy.

Some people don't give up easily. That's their prerogative. But without violating any of the rules above, give yourself permission to be just as pushy as they are. They'll respect you for it. You can make light of it if you want: "I know you don't give up easily—but neither do I. I'm getting better at saying no."

### 6. Practice.

Choose some easy, low-risk situations in which to practice saying no. Say no when a waiter offers you dessert. Say no when someone tries to sell you something on the street. Go into a room by yourself, shut the door, and say no out loud ten times. It sounds crazy, but building your no muscle helps.

### 7. Establish a preemptive no.

We all have certain people in our lives who tend to make repeated, sometimes burdensome requests of us. In those cases, it's better to say no before the request even comes in. Let that person know that you're hyper-focused on a couple of things in your life and trying to reduce your obligations in all other areas. If it's your boss who tends to make the requests, agree upfront with her about where you should be spending your time. Then, when the requests come in, you can refer to your earlier conversation.

### 8. Be prepared to miss out.

Some of us have a hard time saying no because we hate to miss an opportunity. And saying no always leads to a missed opportunity. But it's not just a missed opportunity; it's a trade-off. Remind yourself that when you're saying no to the request, you are simultaneously saying yes to something you value more than the request. Both are opportunities. You're just choosing one over the other.

## 9. Gather your courage.

If you're someone who is used to saying yes, it will take courage to say no, especially if the person asking doesn't give up easily. You may feel like a bad friend, or like you're letting someone down or not living up to expectations. Maybe you'll imagine that you'll be seen or talked about in a negative light. Those things might be the cost of reclaiming your life. You'll need courage to put up with them.

After Irene tried these practices, she started working less and spending more time with her kids. She's still doing great work and she's still valued by her boss and coworkers.

They're respecting her boundaries—they don't even seem to resent her for them—but she's had to give up something she never knew was important to her: her sense of herself as someone who could do it all. It's been hard for her to feel as valued and necessary as she did when she always said yes.

"Would you rather go back to saying yes all the time?" I asked her. She answered me with a very well-practiced no.

> For many of us, our instinctual response to a request is to say yes. But in a world that will take what it can from us, graciously saying no is the way to stay both productive and sane. Preserve your bond with the other person by saying no to the request, while saying yes to the relationship.

• • • •

# 34 Towing Our Neighbor's Son's Car

## Ask Questions.
## Don't Attack Back.

ELEANOR AND I USED TO LIVE IN AN APARTMENT BUILDING DEDI-cated to faculty and staff of Princeton University. Leslie, a very intense economics professor, lived in the apartment above us. Tall, smart, strong willed, and opinionated, Leslie had a reputation on campus for being aggressive. We had a cordial relationship with her, but she intimidated us.

Each apartment came with a single, designated parking space, and one night, Eleanor and I returned home from a late movie to find an unfamiliar car parked in our space. It was after midnight, and with no owner in sight and nowhere nearby to legally park our car, we had the car towed, parked our car in its place, and went to sleep.

The next morning there was a loud knock on the door. Eleanor—to her dismay—was the first to answer.

It was Leslie, her body tense, her hands balled into fists, her face beet red. The moment she saw Eleanor, she unleashed a barrage of angry words and accusations. I was in the back of the apartment and could hear her clearly.

"How could you have done that to me?" she screamed. "I can't believe you could be so obnoxious!"

It turns out the mystery car we had towed belonged to her son. "He hates Princeton," Leslie screamed, "because it's filled with mean, self-centered people, and now you've confirmed his prejudices."

Eleanor, usually calm and collected, responded instinctively, "Did you just call us mean and self-centered?" she retorted. "It's *our* parking space, and he was in it! And you're screaming at me! You're calling *us* mean and self-centered?"

This only made Leslie angrier and louder. They went at it, both arguing their points, getting more enraged, and entrenching more deeply in their positions. The conversation was spiraling down, yet neither of them could stop or change it's direction. The longer they argued, the farther they moved from any useful, positive resolution.

As I listened from the back of the house, I had a quiet—though admittedly adrenaline-filled—moment to consider what to do. My impulse was to jump in, defend our actions, yell louder if I had to, and win the fight since I was convinced we did nothing wrong. But I resisted that temptation. Ultimately, I want a good relationship with our neighbor, and that for sure, would not have gotten us there.

Instead, I asked myself, What does Leslie want from us?

The answer was immediately obvious to me—since she was yelling, that must mean she wanted to be heard. Once she felt we understood her point of view and appreciated how angry she was, I bet she would calm down. Then we could talk. If I wanted to have a productive conversation with Leslie, I needed to defuse her anger first. So, rather than fight, I had to listen.

But I felt like I needed a way in. Something before listening that would clearly indicate my interest to be in a real conversation with her. I also had real questions as to what was going on. Given that, my next move became obvious to me: ask Leslie questions, and try to understand where she was coming from.

To do that, I needed to ask open-ended, exploratory questions: who, what, when, where, how, why, and the like—questions that would clarify what she was saying and feeling and help me unpack the situation from her perspective. I would stay away from leading questions and statements that pretended to be questions but wouldn't fool anyone, like "You don't actually believe that, do you?" After asking questions, I would listen and ask follow-up questions to make sure I really understood the situation—not to manipulate her, but because I was really interested in understanding her.

With a plan for how to defuse Leslie's anger, I felt as ready as I was going to be. My heart beat hard as I walked to the doorway where they were standing yelling at each other.

"Hi Leslie," I broke in, "I see you're really angry. What's going on?"

She saw a new victim and pounced. "Angry doesn't even *begin* to describe it . . ." It was hard to simply stand there and listen, but I did. And I asked questions. And listened some more. I wasn't just doing it to placate her; I was doing it to better understand what was going on for her.

It worked. Eventually, I felt like I really understood why she was so angry.

After several minutes, I said, "I want to make sure I understand this right: Your son only visits once in a blue moon, and you really want him to have a good experience when he's with you. And then the people who you think are your good neighbors have his car towed. Not only does it feel like we betrayed you, but we've just given your son one more reason not to come home. I see why you're angry—I would be angry too."

"Yeah, that's right," she said, a little more softly. And then . . . nothing. She was silent. She had nothing left to say. I had understood the depth of her reaction. Her emotional transaction was complete. She felt heard.

At that point, I had enough space in the conversation to tell her we were sorry and that because her son came so rarely, we didn't recognize his car. And since he didn't leave a note on it, we had no way of knowing it was his. And since it was after midnight—too late to go knocking on everyone's doors just to see if the car might belong to them—we made the best decision we could make at the time. Still, we were sorry to have towed her son's car. And we were sorry that he visited so infrequently.

There was a silent pause as we both stood there. Then, to our surprise, she smiled.

"Thank you," she said. And she apologized for her son parking in our space without leaving a note. She also apologized for yelling.

The only reason I was effective in that situation is that I had a minute to think. But while I'm a big believer in pausing before responding, it's hard to do that in the blur of an attack. If I had answered the door instead of Eleanor, I would have reacted even more defensively than she had. That's the knee-jerk reaction that doesn't work: defensiveness, argumentativeness, yelling.

When people learn a martial art, they practice the same move endlessly until it becomes automatic and available when they are ambushed. I realized that day that I needed the conversational equivalent. So I resolved to make a change. I created a new habit when I feel attacked: asking a question.

Whenever I'm surprised and I don't know what to say, I now ask a question. Even if that question is "Can you tell me more?" That gets the other person talking, and in a difficult conversation, it's always useful to let the other person go first. It reduces their defensiveness, you might learn something that could change your perspective or at least help you frame your perspective so they may hear it, and you'll provide an example of good listening they might just follow.

That night we heard a knock on our door, and we both jumped. "Your turn," Eleanor said. It was Leslie again. She asked if we wanted to grab a bite to eat.

Startled by her gesture, I responded instinctively, "What did you have in mind?"

> Whenever you're taken by surprise or feel attacked by someone, resist the impulse to act defensively. Instead ask a question. It is much more likely that the situation will be diffused, and you'll save the time wasted arguing and recriminating.

• • • •

# PART THREE

# Optimize Your Work Habits

n parts 1 and 2, I shared how four seconds is all the time you need to replace damaging habits with ones that help you connect with yourself and with others. Now the challenge is to take one more step to fully use all your power: to engage in behaviors that help you work and lead in a way that inspires you and inspires others to follow you and do their best.

Remember the flood in my kitchen? After Sophia, Daniel, and I cleaned up the mess, our job was not done. I sat both kids down and asked them what else needed to happen.

"You're going to punish us?" Sophia asked.

"Nope," I said. "I think you guys know what went wrong, and I'm confident it won't happen again."

"So nothing else needs to happen." Daniel said, hopefully.

"Nope again." I said, "Who else might be affected by this flood?"

It took them a few minutes, but with my help, they figured out that the water may have leaked into our downstairs neighbors' apartment.

"So, what should we do about it?" I asked.

"We should go down there and see it!" Daniel said, clearly excited by the novelty.

"And . . . ?" I asked

"And apologize?" Sophia said.

So we walked downstairs to speak with our neighbors and took responsibility for the flood (it had, in fact, leaked into their apartment). We apologized and asked if we could help them clean up the mess. They were gracious and appreciative that we had come down.

We have a dual responsibility at work and as leaders: to achieve particular outcomes and to foster engaged and independently capable people and teams. It's much easier to do one and forget the other—to achieve our objectives while leaving other people behind, or to bring others along but fail to achieve what we set out to accomplish.

When my kids flooded the kitchen, I had those two goals in mind: fix the damage and engage them while developing their skills for the future. Taking that breath and resisting the urge to yell at them (part 1), connecting with them and seeing what they needed (part 2), and then engaging them in taking responsibility (part 3) is what leadership is all about.

In part 3, you'll learn to subvert the knee-jerk reactions that either bowl people over in order to get stuff done, or that tiptoe around their feelings and get nothing done. You'll learn to overcome the temptation to do things that lead to negativity, and you'll learn how to instead help people commit to, and follow through on, the actions that will make a difference to your most important objectives. You'll learn to behave in ways that create the space for people to collaborate, change, and blossom. You will discover

- why you can't counter negativity with positivity, and a strategy for turning bad attitudes into good ones;

- why taking credit for results can backfire, but giving credit can get you acknowledged;

- how taking responsibility for someone else's failure can be the most powerful leadership move you can make;

- why people don't resist change but do resist the way we often lead it; and why willpower and discipline are unreliable strategies for sustaining high performance, and a strategic approach to replace them.

As you read the chapters in part 3, you will begin to stand more powerfully in your work and your leadership, acting in ways that routinely and predictably help you, and the people around you, achieve the outcomes you want.

# 35 Hair Salon Leadership

## Keep Your Cool

**I LAY BACK IN THE CHAIR, CLOSED MY EYES, AND ALMOST IMMEDI-**
ately felt my body relax. An instant later, a stream of warm water
rinsed through my hair while strong, competent hands massaged
my scalp. For that moment, my stress disappeared, washed away
with the water.

I might as well have been at some exotic spa on vacation in the
Caribbean, but I was in New York City, in the middle of a workday, still in my suit, getting my hair cut. After the shampoo, in a
slight daze of tranquility, I was guided to a chair and Avi, the
owner of the salon, began to cut my hair. We started to chat when,
suddenly, behind us, a commotion started. I watched Avi in the
mirror as he looked around to see what was happening.

One of the other hairstylists, Jon, was talking to a colleague,
gesturing dramatically, clearly upset. The other customers began
to look around, a little uncomfortable, not sure what was happening. Avi excused himself and went over to Jon. He spoke softly to
him and listened, and in a few seconds, Jon calmed down.

Avi returned to my haircut, apologized again, made a joke—
but not at Jon's expense—and resumed his cutting.

"So Avi," I said, "You know I've gotta ask, What was that about?"

It turns out that Jon had gotten into a small dispute with a client on the phone. The client had asked Jon to spend the day doing her hair at her wedding but was upset by the fee he quoted, which was much higher than a single haircut. He tried to explain to her that he'd have to give up a day's work at the salon and needed to cover that lost work. Still, she was upset and that made him upset—a little dramatic.

Which, Avi said, must never happen in his salon.

"Drama?" I asked.

"Anything unprofessional. We're always on stage. We're all in a single open space. Anything anyone does is visible to everyone else. I don't want customers, other stylists, the receptionist—anyone—to feel uncomfortable."

That's when it hit me: We all work in a hair salon.

I was recently on the trading floor of a large bank. Hundreds of people were sitting next to each other in rows, everyone visible to everyone else. The head of the department, one of the top ten people leading this multibillion-dollar company, worked in an office constructed entirely of glass. There was no place to hide.

And it's not just trading floors. Many of the newly built offices I've seen are built as open spaces with everyone from the CEO to the receptionist visible to everyone. Even in older buildings almost everyone sits in cubicles or behind glass walls. This architectural style reflects a management style—we're breaking down the walls between us, trying to soften the hierarchy, and offering transparency. It also reflects a social style facilitated by the Internet that exposes, well, just about everything.

In other words, there's no place to hide.

In the past, we could be calm and professional in front of everyone and then walk into our private offices and lose it. That harmless venting didn't impact anyone. But when our offices are glass—or worse, desks in the middle of everyone else—our losses of composure are losses of professionalism. People begin to lose confidence and trust in us.

So when Avi noticed Jon lose his composure, he knew two things: (1) everyone was looking at Jon, and (2) everyone was wondering what Avi would do about it. Avi passed the test. He maintained his composure, spoke softly to Jon, and let Jon know that it would be better if he as the salon owner—not Jon—negotiated the price. He promised that he would do just that after my haircut.

"When you're in charge," Avi told me, "you need to look good, relaxed, in control. Meanwhile your stomach is turning because you see that things aren't running like they're supposed to."

Avi demonstrated the new rules of professionalism in an open workplace. We all have a natural tendency to vent—but in today's work environments, it's almost impossible to vent in a way that isn't destructive to you and the people around you. If you feel uncontrollably emotional, write in a journal as angrily as you want. Or go into the bathroom alone and have a tantrum. Or go for a walk.

But, in public, be calm. Be supportive of others. Show leadership by avoiding—and, when necessary, actively managing—drama that could distract, embarrass, or unsettle others. And never, ever be the cause of that drama yourself.

"You know," Avi said to me. "Hair stylists can be a little, well, fragile and moody. You need to handle them gently. Otherwise they'll just leave."

He's right. But it's not just hairstylists. It's people. We're all a little fragile and at times, moody. We all need to be handled with care. I emerged from the salon an hour after I had entered with a great haircut, more relaxed then I had been in a long time. And that led me to one final insight.

If you're in a situation in which your professionalism is hard to maintain—for some reason you've become upset, riled up, or anxious—and a deep breath or glass of water isn't enough, go for a walk. Leave the office—or whatever space you're in—entirely. Then, if you have the time, walk over to your neighborhood hair salon and ask for a shampoo and cut. You'll emerge composed, relaxed, and professional.

> Resist the natural tendency to vent at work. If you feel uncontrollably emotional, upset, or riled up, leave the situation. We need to be diligent and disciplined about how we act because, as Avi observed, we're always on stage.

• • • •

# 36 George Washington vs. Super Bowl I

## See Individuals Individually

"I'VE ALWAYS BEEN A STATS GUY," DON STEINBERG WROTE IN THE *Philadelphia Inquirer*,[11] explaining why he invented America Bowl, a contest pitting Presidents against Super Bowls to see which is better.

The year his article came out, there had been forty-four presidents in U.S. history, and it was the forty-fourth Super Bowl game. "America Bowl will match a President against the same-numbered Super Bowl game," Don described on his website. "Each day one will win—and score a point." For example, on the first day of the contest, George Washington was compared to Super Bowl I. George won. Presidents: 1; Super Bowls: 0.

"Which have been better?" Don asks, "Our Super Bowl games? Or our Presidents? Finally, we can find out!"

Crazy, right? I mean, how can you compare a President to a Super Bowl? That's not apples and oranges, it's apples and orangutans. That is, of course, why it's funny and why, according to the *Economist*, it's "a delightful way to waste time."

Yet many of us spend hours a day comparing ourselves to those around us. How does our work compare? How does our business compare? How do our bank accounts, our looks, our children compare? And we don't just compare ourselves to others, we compare others to each other, like when we rank our employees or compare people on our teams.

But if everybody does it, can comparing really be such a bad habit?

Yes, in fact, it can, because (a) it's impossible to do it right, and (b) when you try, you create a tremendous amount of damage.

(A) *Why is comparing impossible?*

Consider the Winter Olympics. The racers in the men's downhill skiing competition are ranked based on one, simple criterion: their time. That's a great use of ranking. Same idea with the women's ice hockey competition: the team that scores the most points wins the game, which is another good example of ranking.

But now, how about we compare the male downhill racers with the female ice hockey players and rank them based on who performs better?

It's impossible, of course, because they're playing different games. So how can we rank Bill from Accounting and Jane from Sales? And even if we keep the ranking within a particular department, jobs are often sufficiently different within the same area that performance is unrankable. Can you compare the downhill racers with slalom racers? They're both ski racers, but their competitions are incomparable. That's why they have separate gold medals and more often than not, different winners.

Ultimately, comparing misses the basic and very human principle of talent management: each person is unique. Great managers maximize the impact of each person's unique talents to make a positive impact. They understand each one of their employees well enough to put him or her in the exact role, the exact situation, that leverages the individual's exceptional strengths and mitigates the negative consequences of the person's distinctive weaknesses. They don't waste energy comparing one person to another. They focus energy by comparing each person to the particular job he or she is tasked to accomplish. Unless everyone is doing the exact same thing in the exact same way—which rarely happens—it's a waste of time to compare them. It's worse than a waste of time; it's destructive mismanagement.

(B) *So comparing can't be done. But why is trying to do it so damaging?*

When I assess the strengths of a CEO's leadership team, I look, more than anything, at how they work together. Do senior leaders take responsibility for companywide problems even if the problems have nothing to do with their particular business? Are they willing to sacrifice the success of their division or region in order to support the success of the larger organization?

That's teamwork for a greater good. It's exactly the kind of teamwork that makes a manager succeed over time and exactly the kind of teamwork that ranking discourages. Can we really expect people to help each other succeed when they know they'll be paid more if the people around them fail?

People learn by taking risks, reaching outside their comfort zone, stepping into roles that are too big, making mistakes and correcting them. That means their performance *will* go down if they're learning. But rank people and you end up penalizing them for taking on more challenges. In other words, you're effectively telling people, "If you want to get paid well, stop learning." Can we really expect people to take on challenging tasks if we pay them less for doing so?

"I never figured my nutty 'America Bowl' would catch fire the way it has." Don Steinberg said.

If only we can stop the fire from spreading to corporations.

> Comparing—yourself to others or others to each other—doesn't get you anywhere. Each person has a unique blend of skills, motivations, passions, capabilities, strengths, weaknesses, character, and personality. Seeing individuals individually will elicit better performance, loyalty, and gratitude.

● ● ● ●

# 37 Complaining with Complainers

## Neutralize Negativity

"I'M GETTING TO THE END OF MY PATIENCE," DAN, THE HEAD OF sales for a financial services firm, told me. "There is so much opportunity here—the business is growing, the work is interesting, and bonuses should be pretty good this year—but all I hear is complaining."

When he passed his employees in the hall and asked how it was going, they would respond with a critical comment about a client, or they would grumble about the amount of work they were juggling.

"How can I turn around the negativity that pervades my team?" he asked me.

I asked him what he was doing now. "At first, I told them how much opportunity we had in front of us, and I reiterated our mission statement," he said. "I wanted to remind them what we're all working towards. Now though?" he threw his hands up in the air, "I'm just pissed. I want to shake them out of their slump."

Both of Dan's responses are completely natural and intuitive. Unfortunately, they are also completely ineffective. First, he tried to counter the negativity with positivity. When that didn't work, he became negative himself. Both responses reaped the same outcome: more negativity.

Here's why: countering someone's negativity with your positivity doesn't work because it's argumentative. People don't like to be emotionally contradicted, and if you try to convince them that they shouldn't feel something, they'll only feel it more stubbornly. And if you're a leader trying to be positive, it comes off even worse because you'll appear out of touch and aloof to the reality that people are experiencing.

The other instinctive approach—confronting someone's negativity with your own negativity—doesn't work because it's additive. Your negative reaction to their negative reaction simply adds fuel to the fire. Negativity breeds negativity.

So how can you turn around negativity?

I discovered the answer when I made Dan's mistake with Eleanor when she was complaining about our kids fighting. At first, I tried to convince her that all kids fight and ours weren't so bad. Then I became frustrated with her complaining and told her as much. She got angry. Who wouldn't? But then she did something really helpful for me: she told me what she needed from me.

"I don't want to feel that I'm alone in this," she said. "I want to know you understand. I want you to tell me that we're in this together. And if you share my frustrations, I want to know that too."

In fact, I did share her frustrations, but I was trying not to be negative—which, of course, made the whole interaction more negative. After my conversation with Eleanor, I had a surprising insight: You don't need to change your response. You just need to redirect it.

What Dan had done with his employees is respond negatively against them ("I want to shake them out of their slump") and positively against them ("I told them how much opportunity we had in front of us"). But a much more productive response is to respond negatively *with* others and positively *with* them.

Here's what I'm suggesting, translated into a three-step process for effectively turning around negative people:

### 1. Understand how they feel and validate it.

This might be hard because it could feel like you're reinforcing their negative feelings. But you're not. You're not agreeing with them or justifying their negativity. You're simply showing them that you understand how they feel.

### 2. Find a place to agree with them.

You don't have to agree with everything they've said, but if you can, agree with some of what they're feeling. If you share some of their frustrations, let them know which.

### 3. Find out what they are positive about and reinforce it.

I'm not suggesting you try to convince them to be positive. I'm suggesting you give attention to whatever positive feelings they do show—and chances are they will have shown some because it's unusual to find people who are purely negative. If they are purely negative, then make sure they see you supporting others who have shown positivity. The idea is to give positive attention to positive feeling and to offer concrete hope—hope based on the actual positive feelings people already have, rather than on positive feelings you think they should have.

During step 3, you are responding *positively* with others, not against them. You are showing them that you support them. And you are showing them that they will be rewarded—with your support and attention—when they do and say things that are positive. During step 3 you are transforming the downward spiral into an upward one. In my conversation with Eleanor, I asked her what has worked in the past to keep the kids playing nicely together. She talked about a previous morning when we directed their attention more proactively by doing an art project with them. It also worked well, she said, when she and I took each kid individually to do an errand or a project.

In less than five minutes, my conversation with Eleanor reversed its course from negative to positive.

These three steps are not easy to do because we have to fight our own highly emotional—and even reasonable—tendency to be negative about people who are complaining. When I initially spoke with Dan, he was ready to fire some of his team. That would have, of course, simply exacerbated the negativity of those who stayed. Instead, he started to listen and validate their negative feelings. What he found underneath the complaining was fear. The company had recently experienced layoffs, and the survivors were still shaken. Were their jobs at risk?

Dan couldn't say that they weren't—especially since he was ready to fire some of the complainers. But what he did do was listen and tell them that he shared some of their anxiety—not about being fired, but about feeling unsettled with so much to accomplish and fewer people to get the job done. In other words, he was negative with them (step 2).

Then he highlighted some positive things he noticed on his team—people taking smart risks, working together on complex

sales, and partnering successfully with clients—that were helping to grow the company and secure people's jobs. In other
words, he was positive with them (step 3).

Before, Dan never missed an opportunity to highlight—and
criticize—a person's negativity. Now he didn't miss an opportunity to highlight—and praise—a person's positivity. And it
worked. Eventually the mood in the sales group turned around,
and they worked together to bring in the largest client the company had ever won.

As for me? In the heat of the moment, I can still get frustrated
with other people's frustrations. But following these three steps
has helped tremendously. And having a partner who reminds me
of them? That helps even more.

> Never meet someone's negativity with your
> positivity. If you want to turn around someone's
> attitude, try agreeing with them first.

• • • •

# 38 The Training Wheels Had to Come Off

## Let People Fail— or Almost Fail

"PUT MY TRAINING WHEELS BACK ON," SOPHIA SAID IN A STERN tone, "or I'm not going to ride my bike!" She had just turned four that day and wanted to learn to ride a bike like her older sister. Now she wasn't so sure.

After a lot of encouraging and a little stubbornness of my own, she was willing to try. We agreed to practice fifteen minutes a day until she got it. A couple of days later, we weren't getting anywhere. It's not that she wasn't trying, it's just that she didn't seem to be able to get her balance on her own.

Then it dawned on me: I was getting in the way. I didn't want my baby girl to get hurt. And I was afraid if she fell she would give up trying completely. So as soon as she tipped to one side— even a little—I caught her. In other words, Sophia still had training wheels on her bike: me. If I wanted her to learn, I had to let go—figuratively and literally. It's not that I planned to let her fall to the ground; it's just that I had to let her fall closer to the ground so that she had the opportunity to catch herself.

Learning to ride a bike—learning anything, actually—isn't about doing it right. It's about doing it wrong and then adjusting. Learning isn't about being in balance; it's about recovering balance. And you can't recover balance if someone keeps you from losing balance in the first place.

So my job got a lot harder. I had to use more refined judgment. Was Sophia falling to the left? Should I reach out before she hit the pavement? Or was she just leaning? Could she steer in the other direction and recover? I had to time my catch just right.

That challenge—timing the catch just right—is the central challenge we face as managers. It's the sweet spot between micromanagement and neglect. Allowing for failure while ensuring the safety of our employees and our companies.

If an employee comes to you with a presentation that doesn't meet your expectations, what do you do? Take it, fix it, and present it yourself? Tell him what he's done wrong and ask him to fix it? Allow him to present it without making changes, and let him face the consequences? Each choice is legitimate in the right circumstances.

Our job is to gauge the circumstances correctly. What's the risk, the consequences of failure? Is time critical? Will mistakes destroy the person's reputation forever? Or will it be an effective learning experience? Once we gauge the circumstances, we can adapt, changing our response to help the employee learn to recover, stay upright, and keep pedaling.

That adaptation is more difficult than it sounds. It means resisting, or at least questioning, our natural tendencies. Because we all have a favorite response when our expectations aren't met. What do you do when you've given direction to an employee and she doesn't follow it?

Maybe you tell her even more clearly what you expect from her and require that she try again. Maybe you ask her what she was thinking and how she plans to approach it next time. Maybe you sit down and do it with her. Maybe you do it yourself. The question is, if you're going to choose a different response, how do you choose?

Here's one way: ask yourself what it will take for the employee to recover herself. How close is she to the ground? Is she falling or simply leaning? What will help her regain her balance? What can you do that will give her that opportunity?

When I was first teaching Sophia to ride her bike, I made all sorts of excuses for her. She was only four; her sister was six when she learned to ride. I wondered if I was pushing her too hard. So my natural tendency was to rescue her.

What I eventually realized was that I was really making excuses for myself. I was afraid of her skinned knee and bruised confidence, so I didn't give her the opportunity to fail, which meant I didn't give her the opportunity to succeed.

As soon as I changed my approach to teaching Sophia—on the third day of our routine—she learned to balance herself while pedaling. The next day she managed to stop by herself, and the day after that she learned to get herself going from a standstill. By the end of the sixth day, she could turn in a figure eight. No training wheels necessary.

> Our natural instinct is to prevent all failure, but doing so stunts growth. Your job as a leader is to build an independently capable team, which means learning when to let people fail and when to catch them.

• • • •

# 39 Are You Ready to Be a Leader?

## Support Others' Success

ONE OF MY CLIENTS, BARBARA, IS A VERY ACCOMPLISHED TECHNOL-ogist at a financial-services company. She runs a large department and is highly respected. I started working with her because she had been passed over for promotion to managing director several times. She received feedback that she needed to act "more senior."

When I spoke with Barbara she didn't know what "more senior" meant, but she figured she needed more visibility so other people would notice her hard and successful work.

So she began to promote herself. She made sure her colleagues knew about her projects. She kept her manager and others "in the loop." She sent more e-mails updating people on her accomplishments. She stopped eating lunch at her desk and started going out with senior leaders whenever she could. She wasn't obnoxious or extreme about it, but she deliberately sought visibility for herself and her department.

Her approach was sensible, but it had the opposite effect. Without knowing it, she was sending signals that she was junior. Senior people don't try to get visibility for themselves. They try to get visibility for other people. They don't need visibility for themselves; they already have it. They're senior and everyone knows it.

On a plane once, I sat in the dreaded middle seat between a fit man eating a salad and a significantly overweight man eating a South Beach Diet bar. That candy bar is an example of the problem; the man eating it was setting himself up for failure. If you want to be fit, don't do the things that overweight people do to lose weight. Instead, do the things that fit people do to stay fit. Just start acting like you're already a fit person. Eat the salad, not the bar.

The trick to becoming a senior leader is to act like you're *already* a senior leader. Do what senior leaders do *after* they are senior leaders, not what you think you need to do to become a senior leader.

Once she got that distinction, Barbara changed her strategy. She talked up other people, gave them more credit, and tried to get them promoted. She also changed her focus from her department to the larger organization. Effective senior leaders don't prioritize their own departments over other areas; they think about what's good for the firm as a whole.

At one of my client companies, I saw someone in operations push to get raises for his team when the whole company was under a salary freeze. He thought he was being a great proponent of his people, but his managers saw that he didn't understand the whole company's perspective. They saw him as junior and worse, as not a team player.

At another client company, the new head of a region kept pushing for the needs of that region, even at the expense of the overall firm. Again, that seems reasonable. After all, as the head of the region, what should he push for? But he was ultimately unsuccessful. If you want to sit around the top leadership table, don't advocate for your area. Understand your area better than anyone, but advocate for the company as a whole even if it hurts your area. That's what senior leaders do.

As a leader, the most effective way to be self-interested is to advocate for the interests of the whole. Rather than think of herself as the head of a team, Barbara began to see herself as responsible for the company.

In the past, she had tried to keep all the star performers on her team working for her, even as they outgrew and got bored with their jobs. Now, she looked for opportunities in other areas of the firm and promoted her best people out of her team so they would continue to grow. In the past, she'd spent more of her time advocating her own opinion, which she thought made her sound knowledgeable. Now she asked more questions and explored other people's perspectives, which made her seem wise and open.

Acting wise actually made her wise. She didn't just appear senior; she became senior, adding real value to her company.

Kurt Vonnegut once said, "We are what we pretend to be, so we must be careful what we pretend to be." He used it as a warning. It's equally useful as advice.

In the next go-around, Barbara was promoted to managing director.

> Though it may seem useful, promoting yourself and your accomplishments or advocating for your team too aggressively often backfires. Supporting the success of others, not just your own or your team's, is a good way to support your success in the long run.

• • • •

# 40 Who Deserves Credit for a Great Movie?

## Share the Glory

I WAS WALKING DOWN MAIN STREET IN PARK CITY, UTAH, DURING the Sundance Film Festival with my friend Allison, a casting director who seemed to know everyone. We stopped to say hello to an actor who was disappointed by the reception he was getting at the festival. "Actors are who really make the movie," he told me. "The script is just black and white on a page. It's the actor who breathes life into the words."

Later, we bumped into another friend of Allison, a writer who had a movie in the festival. He too was feeling dissatisfied, and the conversation was remarkably similar. "A movie is created by the writer," he told us. "It's the writer who invents the story, who's responsible for the film." We didn't speak with a director on that walk, but I'm confident that if we had, we would have heard the claim that films are most influenced by the creative voice of the director.

That walk happened to be down Main Street during Sundance, but it could have been down the corridor in almost any office building during a typical day.

Who is responsible—and should get the most credit—for a product or service that brings in high revenues? The team who designed it? The people who marketed it? The sales force who sold it? The service reps who gave customers the confidence to buy it? The executive leadership team who strategized it?

Not every person on the team is equally valuable, right? Think of a sports team—there are stars, who get paid tens of millions, and then there are the other players, who make, well, a lot less. It's simple supply and demand: some people are more easily replaceable than others.

So, logically, we would have to say that the highest-paid, most-visible, most-irreplaceable people are responsible for the greatness of the product or service. Until we look at the list of Oscar nominees. Let's take 2010 as an example.

What's most interesting about the list isn't which movies were nominated for Best Picture. What's most interesting is what other categories the Best Picture winners were nominated for. Best Picture nominee *Black Swan,* for example, was also nominated for Best Directing, Best Actress in a Leading Role, Best Cinematography, and Best Film Editing. Best Picture nominee *The Fighter* was also nominated for Best Original Screenplay, Best Directing, Best Film Editing, Best Actor in a Supporting Role, and it received two nominations for Best Actress in a Supporting Role. Best Picture nominee *Inception* was also nominated for Best Original Screenplay, Best Art Direction, Best Cinematography, Best Original Score, Best Sound Editing, Best Sound Mixing, and Best Visual Effects. Best Picture nominee *The King's Speech* was nominated for a total of eleven other awards. *True Grit* had nine other nominations. *The Social Network,* seven.

And perhaps most telling, the number of Best Picture nominees with no nominations in other categories? None. In fact, to be nominated for Best Picture, a film had to be best in at least three other categories.

In other words, a movie is only considered great when all the various parts are independently, and collaboratively, great. It's never entirely the talent of a single person or team. It's never even mostly the talent of a single person or team—even when that person is Mark Wahlberg, or Natalie Portman, or a Coen brother.

In total, the ten Best Picture movies were nominated for five directing awards, nine screenplay awards, fifteen acting awards, and twenty-nine other awards. I call these others the back-office awards—like film editing, sound mixing, cinematography, and art direction. It is unlikely that any of these movies would be nominated for Best Picture—and even more unlikely that they would win—if not for the stellar work done by the teams and people we rarely see and almost never acknowledge. We probably don't even know what most of them do.

It is almost always a mistake to highlight an individual, a role, or a team as responsible for the success of a venture in which a group contributes. Those we spoke to at Sundance might have each been correct in thinking that they don't get enough credit. But they were also each wrong in thinking of themselves as deserving the credit.

The best producers—arguably, the CEOs of movies—understand this. I spoke to one highly accomplished producer who told me that the film world highlights directors because, from a PR standpoint, it helps to have a focal point for a movie. Like a brand name for a company. But, he told me, putting all the focus on a great director or a famous actor is clearly not the way to make a great movie. Did you see *The Tourist*? Even Johnny Depp and Angelina Jolie can't save a bad film.

The best leaders know that credit for most any achievement should be spread broadly—they don't just devote lip service to the idea—they really know it to be true. And they convey it through their own humility. Humility isn't just an attitude; it's a skill. The most effective people are highly confident (they know they add significant value) and manifestly humble (they recognize the immense value added by those around them).

At the end of our walk down Main Street in Park City, I turned to my friend Allison and asked her whether she wasn't the most important person in a film because she chose many of the people who would make it successful.

"Oh, I'm important," she told me smiling, then added, "At least as important as everyone else."

> It is almost always a mistake to highlight an individual, a role, or a specific team as responsible for the success of a venture in which a bigger group contributes. Make sure that everyone involved sees themselves as part of the story of success.

● ● ● ●

# 41 The Chef Who Didn't Get It

## Take Responsibility for Your Colleagues' Work

I STEPPED UP TO THE COUNTER AND ORDERED A BAGEL WITH SMOKED salmon and cream cheese. I asked for the sandwich to be open faced, "with salmon on both sides of the bagel so my friend and I can share it."

"No problem," Andrea, the waitress behind the counter, told me. She punched a few buttons on the computer display of her cash register, electronically communicating our special order to the kitchen, and gave me a table stand with a number on it to identify us to the waiter responsible for serving the tables.

About ten minutes later, David, the waiter, brought out the bagel. It was open faced, but all the salmon was on one half of the bagel. The other half just had cream cheese.

No big deal. But the restaurant was nearly empty, and I was curious. "Thanks," I said, "but I had asked for salmon on both sides of the bagel."

David apologized and took it back to the kitchen. A minute later, he came back. This time, the salmon was placed on half of each side of the bagel. The other half was plain cream cheese. Think a salmon and cream cheese yin/yang symbol.

What's most interesting is what David said when he gave me the bagel: "I know this isn't what you wanted," he said, smiling sheepishly. "The chef obviously didn't get it."

Again, just to be clear, this was, of course, no big deal. I thanked him and took the bagel. But questions ran through my head: *If you knew, why didn't you explain it to the chef? When he gave you the bagel and you saw it wasn't what I wanted, why didn't you tell him? Or fix it yourself before bringing it out? And, finally, once you decided to bring it out as is, why blame the chef?*

There's a one-word answer to all those questions: silos.

Andrea's job was to take my order and transmit it to the chef. The chef's job was to create the sandwich. And David's job was to bring out the final dish. In fact, David did his job well. Only it wasn't the right dish.

This obviously isn't just an issue particular to a restaurant. It's an issue that most of us face every day.

Here's the problem: our jobs are complex and interdependent, but our goals, objectives, and most importantly, mindsets, are often siloed.

We each have a job to do—sell a service, design a product, address a customer issue—and the underlying mindset is, If I do my job well, and you do your job well, we'll achieve our goals.

But it rarely works that way. People in one silo often have information needed by—but never given to—people in another silo. And, as my experience in the restaurant showed, if there's a problem anywhere, everyone fails. Who is responsible for my sandwich? Andrea? The chef? David? It's a waste of time to parse that one out. And it's damaging to try. The truth is, they're all, collectively, responsible.

In other words—and this might be hard to swallow—we are responsible for each other's work. Being responsible for each other's work is not about figuring out who deserves the blame. It's about the practical reality of collaboration.

After breakfast, I asked David ("for the sake of an article I'm writing") to spend a few minutes with me exploring his decision making.

"Frankly," David told me, "I work with the chef every day, and I didn't want to be too pushy. I didn't want to make him angry."

In other words, telling the chef that he had gotten the sandwich wrong—that the chef had made a mistake—was threatening to their relationship. It wasn't a risk David wanted to take.

"It was a split-second decision," David continued. "Is it worth a confrontation with the chef or would you guys be okay with the sandwich delivered wrong? You guys seem mellow, and so I chose not to face the chef."

David decided it would be less painful to pass the mistake to the customer than to confront his colleague or superior about it. It would be easy to judge David for making this choice if so many of us didn't make that same decision all the time. So how do we escape the silo mentality?

Courage.

Overcoming our destructive tendency to work through silos requires the courage of a single person willing to take personal risks. It takes great personal strength to identify and help correct a mistake in "someone else's" silo and to overcome the fear of the consequences of taking responsibility for a colleague's work.

When I spoke with David, he agreed that it would have been better if he had said something to the chef. Better for me, better for the restaurant, better for the chef, and even, over time, his relationship with the chef.

"So will you do it?" I asked.

David—a good guy, someone with enough courage to explore his decision making with me honestly—looked over at the kitchen for a second, then back at me, and smiling, he shrugged.

> Resist the temptation to view your job as separate from the jobs of others—that is, as a silo. From the view of a leader, a shareholder, or a customer, there is no such thing as a silo. Take responsibility for your colleagues' work and commit to excellence—not of any one piece—but of the whole.

• • • •

# 42 I've Got Too Much to Do . . .

## Offer to Do Other People's Work

I KNOW HOW TO HANDLE STRESS. I KNOW THAT EACH DAY I NEED TO get seven or eight hours of sleep and an hour or so of exercise. I know I need to meditate for a few minutes and eat normal-sized, well-balanced meals. I know I need to take deep, calming breaths throughout the day. I know all this, and for the most part (disregarding the second bowl of chocolate chips mixed with peanut butter and Rice Krispies I just devoured), I do those things.

And yet, even knowing—and doing—the right things to manage stress effectively, I'm still stressed. Almost overwhelmingly.

The work-related things that are stressing me this week are on top of the normal demands of life—raising three children, each with their unique set of blessings and challenges; making time for an amazing wife who has stresses of her own; and growing my own business. These are all good stresses to have. I'm healthy, my family is healthy, my business is healthy, and our finances are healthy.

But stress doesn't discriminate between good and bad. It comes, unbidden, anytime we are in a situation in which we are worried about an outcome we feel is beyond our control. So we complain. We gossip. We get snarky. Quickly our stress infects those around us. And then they complain, gossip, and get snarky. Pretty soon, we're competing for who's most stressed, who's got the most work, or who's got the most ungrateful, unreasonable boss. Of course, that just makes us all more stressed. What is the best way to cope with feeling overwhelmed while also managing the complaining, gossiping, snarky colleague? How should we respond without becoming that person ourselves?

Offer to do some of their work for them.

I know it sounds crazy because you're already so busy—probably busier than they are. Even if you did have the time and energy to help them, you might not be feeling so generous toward them because all of their complaining is annoying. On top of that, if you're competing for who's the busiest, how will it look to offer to do their work? You'll lose that battle for sure.

But you'll win the war on stress.

We complain because we feel alone and disconnected in our stress. So we gossip to create camaraderie with our fellow gossiper. We get snarky about our boss to align ourselves with our colleague. But complaining and gossiping are like my chocolate-chip and peanut-butter Rice Krispies mixture—they make us feel good while we're doing it, but we feel worse immediately afterward.

Complaining breeds distrust with our colleagues, it infuses the office with negativity, it wastes time, and it solidifies our sense of isolation. Offering to take some of their work, on the other hand, achieves the opposite; it creates connection, which, ultimately, is what we're after.

If someone were really in serious trouble—think of the people in Japan after the tsunami—we wouldn't hesitate to reach out and help. Think of this as that same, generous, human response only on a much smaller, less critical scale. The unexpected offer will immediately change the dynamic. Who would continue to complain in the face of an offer to share the burden? It builds trust, creates a positive work atmosphere, and gets things done.

It also helps you get your own work done. Reaching out in an act of generosity makes you feel better and moves you away from your stress and toward your productivity. By acting as if you have the capacity to help someone out, you actually gain that capacity.

So how should you do it?

*Listen without contributing or competing.* Empathize with the other person's challenge. Resist the temptation to join in, add your own juicy piece of gossip, or talk about how much work you have and how hard it is for you, too. Just listen.

*Acknowledge the challenge she is facing.* In one or two short sentences, let them know that you understand they're in a tough, stressful spot. Don't patronize; don't add on. This might be hard if you feel like you're in a tough spot, too, but you don't need to agree with what they're saying. You just need to convey that you hear what they're saying.

*Offer to help in a specific way.* Maybe they're dreading a conversation with someone and you can offer to intervene on their behalf. Maybe you can help them out in a personal way like grabbing lunch for them when you get your own, saving them the trip. Don't worry that they might become dependent on your doing their work for them. Sure there's a risk they might take you for granted. But, more likely, they'll be appreciative, stop complaining, and you'll both get to work with renewed energy. Next time, they might even do the same for you, which is how a great, productive team operates.

The other night, I fell into the trap of complaining to Eleanor about how busy and stressed I was, even though I knew how busy and stressed she was. She didn't compete. She listened, told me she could see how stressed I was, and then, even though the next day was my morning with the kids, she offered to wake up with them at 6 A.M. while I slept a little later. It completely changed the dynamic. I stopped complaining and immediately realized how fortunate I am. Later that next day when she needed time to do some work, I offered to cover for her, which made me feel even better than sleeping late.

Now you may be thinking: *This is your wife; of course she should help you. You two are partners in life. The way we manage workloads with our colleagues is different.* But does it need to be? Why can't we take small steps at work to share an individual's load in the interest of the well-being of the team?

I'm still super busy. I still have all these obligations that are hanging over me. Nothing material has changed. And yet everything has changed. Because even though I'm singularly responsible for achieving my obligations, somehow, I don't feel alone in them.

Our reaction to feeling stressed about how much work we have is often competitive complaining. But while it makes us feel good for a short while, it ignites a spiral of negativity into the workplace and our day. Instead, flip it around by offering to help someone else with their work. Reaching out in an act of generosity will make you feel better and move you away from your stress and toward your productivity.

● ● ● ●

# 43 The Day the Distribution Centers Were Full

## Focus on Outcome, Not Process

DURING THE WEEKS AND MONTHS SURROUNDING HURRICANE Sandy, the storm that devastated parts of New York City, the city could have been described as, not one city, but two: one of people who were drastically impacted by Hurricane Sandy, and another of those who were merely inconvenienced by it.

I am fortunate: I live on the Upper West Side of Manhattan, which was minimally affected. Our kids were out of school for several days, but we never lost power, and our apartment suffered no damage. We also own a car, which we filled with gas the night of the storm, just in case.

So when we received several e-mails announcing an effort to collect and deliver supplies to some hard-hit neighborhoods, we were prepared to help. By the time I arrived at the Jewish Community Center in Manhattan, its lobby was piled high with clothing, food, toys, toiletries, blankets, flashlights, and other necessities, all packed in black garbage bags. There were people to sort, people to pack cars, and a leader who was sending people to designated distribution spots in the hardest hit areas. They had already sent a hundred cars filled with supplies and by the end of the day, they sent over a hundred more.

Isabelle and Sophia joined me to take part in the distribution effort. It took volunteers about sixty seconds to fill our minivan and send us on our way to Staten Island.

Then I got a call from a friend who told me not to go to Staten Island. The distribution centers were full, he said. Go to Far Rockaway instead. Several hours of traffic later, when we got to Far Rockaway, the distribution center was already maxed out. So we went to a church we heard was acting as a distribution center. Again, we were turned away—they had as many supplies as they could handle. We found a third, bigger distribution center but were turned away again.

As we slowly drove through Far Rockaway looking for distribution centers, we witnessed devastation of a kind I have never seen. Entire blocks of houses destroyed by fire, with only the front steps standing, leading to charred rubble. Sand and debris—including entire boats—strewn on the streets, left by receding waters. And mounds of discarded wood, furniture, toys, even walls piled high at the curbs for the sanitation department to pick up.

I simply could not believe that the people in these neighborhoods had all the supplies they needed. And yet, here we were, a car filled with supplies but without a distribution center to give them to. That's when I realized the problem: All this coordination was invaluable—to a point. It got our car to the right place, filled with the right things. But now? Now the coordination was getting in the way. I can't quite explain the enormity of this mind shift except to say that with this realization, I shifted from an employee to an entrepreneur. I stopped doing what I was told to do and started doing what I saw needed to be done.

Too often we're placed—or we place ourselves—in the role of cog within a system. We wait for leadership or a bureaucracy to tell us what to do instead of finding out for ourselves what needs to get done. Many of us are instinctively too efficient and follow a process without stopping and really assessing whether that process is helping us achieve our objectives. Sometimes, we lose productivity in an attempt to be productive.

During our search to be helpful, I had to change my process since the old one wasn't moving me forward the way I wanted. I learned that sometimes we need to subvert our desire to be productive and follow processes and instead focus on the outcome and do what it takes to achieve it.

What I also discovered is that when you follow your entrepreneurial initiative, you often end up receiving unexpected gifts. Driving down a random street, we found a number of people clearing debris from their houses. That's where we met Mike and Kelly. Their just refinished basement had flooded to the ceiling like a pool, the water level rose so high it completely submerged and totaled their two cars and, after their son had three asthma attacks from all the dust, they finally sent him to stay with his grandmother in Westchester.

Yes, they told us, we could really use your supplies. And so could others on this street. So we all worked together to unload our car onto Mike's porch where he said he would distribute things to his neighbors.

Mike and Kelly described the night Hurricane Sandy came and the loud bang when the water broke through the basement wall. Kelly took the time to teach my kids about the ocean and the bay—how the water came from both sides and flooded everything. She talked about how they were sharing food with neighbors and trying to help each other in the cleanup. And she gave my kids way more leftover Halloween candy than I approved of.

As I heard about Mike and Kelly's devastation as well as their courage, I felt the blessing of the organizational breakdown. Without coordination, I never would have gotten to Far Rockaway with a minivan full of necessities. But had it all worked smoothly, my kids and I would have given it all to a nameless bureaucracy and never would have met Mike and Kelly and heard their story. And they would never have met us or had the opportunity to tell us their story.

New York City is not two cities; it's eight million cities. This hurricane affected each one of us in a particular way. And to reach across the darkened neighborhoods, debris-strewn streets, and waterlogged houses to hear those stories was a critical—and inspiring—step in the recovery.

Yes, food and clothing and blankets are necessary for survival. But so are the conversations, connections, and sense of community that come from real people sharing with other real people. Those are things we're losing as we distance ourselves from each other in large organizations and efficient modes of communication—as our digital lives overwhelm our in-person ones. We don't have to lose them—after all, organizations are made of people. But the more we act like employees, operating to get the job done as efficiently as possible, the less human we become.

Sharing supplies and stories with neighbors is inefficient. Maybe Mike and Kelly will end up with things on their porch that they can't use and can't give away. Maybe they weren't the people who needed the supplies the most.

But our trip to Far Rockaway helped me see the usefulness of that inefficiency. How much better is it for a neighborhood when one neighbor tells the others to come to his front porch and take what they need instead of signing up for necessities through a distribution center? At first, I'm embarrassed to admit, I'd had the thought, What if they keep it all for themselves? That's precisely the mistrust that leads to—and emerges from—impersonal bureaucracies.

The truth is they might keep it all for themselves.

But I doubt it. Mike and Kelly are good people; that was clear from the way they treated me and my kids. As soon as we arrived at their house, Kelly offered us some of their limited supply of bottled water. They'll take what they need and share what they can.

As we drove back home late that night, we felt great. Not just because we helped out a neighborhood that could use the help. And not just because we tapped into our entrepreneurial initiative, which we were proud of. But also because we met Mike and Kelly and connected with them.

That, it turns out, is the upside of inefficiency.

> Overcome your impulse to be disciplined and follow processes, especially if they don't appear to be working. Instead focus on the outcome and what you need to do to achieve it.

• • • •

# 44  Don't Bet on Winning the Lottery

## Zero In on What Matters to the Organization

MY FRIEND DAVE MENTIONED TO ME THAT HE JUST RECEIVED THE results from a medical exam and was surprised and disappointed by his numbers. His cholesterol was high. Especially, he told me, given how he eats.

"Dave," I said, "you can't be serious. You eat horribly. Everything you eat is fried. And if it's not, then it's a chocolate-chip cookie. I can't remember seeing you eat a vegetable. How can you expect your cholesterol to be anything other than high?"

"But the day before the test," he answered, "I ate really well."

The idea of immediate results is alluring. It's the temptation of the lottery. Who among us hasn't played at least once, imagining how many of our problems could be solved in a moment? Can Dave be faulted for expecting the internal workings of his body to change based on a single day of healthy eating?

Yet instant results are almost always unattainable. And hoping for them is destructive, since it usually prevents us from taking the meaningful, challenging steps that will actually get us to the outcomes we're seeking. Sure, someone wins the lottery. But it's so unlikely to be you that, statistically speaking, your chance is zero.

I was reminded of all this when responding to a reporter about what advice I would give to someone who wanted to ask for a raise at a time when wages were stagnating or falling. My answer? Don't ask.

It's not that I think people can't get raises right now, but if you haven't spent the last year laying the groundwork, it's highly unlikely that you'll be successful. There's no formula—no perfect words or positioning—that will magically deliver a raise with a day or two of preparation. And, when we ask for raises without having done the proper preparation, we hurt ourselves and our reputation, making it even harder to get a raise, even when we deserve one.

But there is a formula for getting more money and growing your career over time. And if you start now, it can position you to get a raise next year.

The formula is based on one simple premise: our careers will progress when we demonstrate that we've added more value. And we can add more value when we spend the majority of our time focusing on the work that the most senior leaders in the organization—or the board—consider valuable. That is almost always work that increases revenue or profits, either short term or long term.

But aren't we already doing this to the best of our ability? I think the deck is stacked against us. We're all overloaded, working on too many things. Answering too many e-mails that don't matter. Offering opinions that aren't necessary. Spending time on issues whose outcomes we can't impact. Doing work that's more bureaucratic than beneficial. There's no question that we're all busier than ever before, but we often are not getting the most important things done.

There are always some things that are more important to do than other things. The problem is that most of us aren't clear about what those are, so one of two things happens: either we put the same amount of energy and effort into everything, or we let the wrong things fall through the cracks.

Minimizing that noise is our opportunity. Here's my formula:

1.  During this year's compensation conversation, take whatever is given to you without negotiation. If it's appropriate, acknowledge that it's been a hard year, and voice your appreciation for what's been offered. Explain that you are less interested in a raise right now and more interested in how you can add tremendous value in the organization—that's what you want to talk about.

2.  Think like a shareholder of the company. Ask lots of questions about the strategy, what's keeping the top leaders awake at night, how your department impacts revenue or profitability, and what's important to your direct manager. Identify, with your manager, the top two or three things you can work on that will drive revenue or profitability. Once you've had that conversation, you'll have your raise-worthy work focus.

3.  Now keep those two or three things on the top of your to-do list. Make sure that the majority of your effort moves the organization further in those areas. Share your to-do list with your manager, making sure that the two of you stay on the same page about what's important and how it's impacting the organization. Do everything you can to quantify the impact you're making. If your

manager starts asking you to do things outside the top two or three things, push back and have a conversation about it. Sure, you'll need to work on some things that aren't important. But make a strategic choice to shortchange those. Do just enough to get by on them; they don't really matter anyway.

Don't make the mistake of asking for a raise without doing the work of finding out what matters to the organization and delivering on those priorities first. Instead, after about six months of this laser focus, you're ready to have a conversation with your manager to identify the impact you've had and prove that you've added tremendous value on the things that matter most. During that discussion you're ready to talk about a real raise. That's good timing since most organizations are beginning to think through their departmental budgets and promotions around the six-month mark.

Here's what's powerful about this formula: it's not a trick; it's in everyone's best interests. If you focus on the things that are most important—even if it requires that you push back against your manager when he or she asks you to work on frivolous things—ultimately you'll be more productive, your manager will be more productive, and the organization will be more productive. That's money in the bank. It will make your job more secure and you more promotable.

"So," I asked Dave. "Now that you know you have high cholesterol, are you going to change the way you eat?"

"No," Dave answered, true to form, "I'm taking a pill. My cholesterol will be lower in a few days, and I can still eat everything."

Maybe I like doing things the hard way. But as far as I know, there's no pill for getting a raise. Still, at a time when wages in most fields are stagnant or falling, it's nice to know at least there's a formula.

It's natural to think the performance review time is the perfect opportunity to ask for a raise. But you need to prepare for that conversation a year in advance, zeroing in on top priorities and delivering on them. Making more intentional and strategic choices about where you spend your time can mean the difference between a stagnant career and a growing one.

•  •  •  •

# 45  Ron Drones On and On

## Be Helpful Instead of Nice

RON WAS UP NEXT. AS A SENIOR ANALYST IN THIS INVESTMENT firm—and a good one—he knew a lot about the company he was about to pitch to the management committee. He paused for a minute as he sorted through the pages of numbers in front of him and then he began to present his case.

Even though Ron described himself as a numbers guy, he seemed to really enjoy this part of his job. He was meticulous in presenting his ideas and took pride in the depth of his analysis. Twenty minutes later, as the meeting ended, James, the head of the firm, thanked him for his work, specifically remarking on his exhaustive research. Ron smiled and thanked James.

Everyone filed out except James and me. I asked him how he thought the meeting went.

"Oh man," he said, "what's the best way to handle an analyst who drones on and on?"

"Who?" I asked. "Ron?"

"He's a great analyst, a smart investor, and a really nice guy. But he talks too much."

"But you told him he did a great job!"

"His analysis was great. But his presentation . . ." He trailed off with a chuckle.

"Have you told him?"

"I've hinted but no, not specifically."

"Why not?"

"I probably should."

But he hasn't. And the reason is simple: James is nice. I know him socially, and he's a delight. I've never seen him do anything that could be remotely construed as mean or rude. And to tell someone that they drone on feels both mean and rude.

But it's neither. It's compassionate.

If we don't provide each other with feedback, we won't become aware of our blind spots. And Ron will continue to drone on and without ever understanding why, lose his audience and his impact.

Giving people feedback is an act of trust and confidence. It shows that you believe in their ability to change, that you believe they will use the information to become better, and that you have faith in their potential. It's also a sign of commitment to the team and to the larger purpose and goals of the organization. Ultimately, we're all responsible for our collective success.

James knows this. And yet even for him—a competent and courageous CEO—it's hard to give someone critical feedback because it still feels aggressive and confrontational. Should you really tell people they talk too much? Or dress poorly? Or appear insincere? Or walk all over others?

Without question, you should.

And not just if you're the CEO. Everyone should offer feedback to everyone else, regardless of position. Because as long as what you say comes from your care and support for the other person—not your sympathy (which feels patronizing) or your power (which feels humiliating) or your anger (which feels abusive)—choosing to offer a critical insight to another is a deeply considerate act.

That doesn't mean that accepting criticism is easy. In the next chapter, you'll read about my own struggles with accepting criticism, and I'll share some tips for being open to learning from critical feedback from others.

But even though giving and accepting feedback may be difficult, letting someone know what everyone else already knows is the opposite of aggressive. Aggressive is not giving people feedback and then talking about them and their issues when they aren't around. Aggressive is watching them fail and not helping.

Ironically, when we avoid sharing feedback, it usually comes out at some point anyway, as gossip or in a burst of anger or sarcasm or blame directed at the person. And *that's* aggressive—passive-aggressive.

On one hand, to avoid that kind of ugliness, it's critical not to delay giving feedback. On the other hand, if we all strutted around willy-nilly tossing criticisms at each other, things would deteriorate quickly. So how should we give feedback?

First, *ask permission.* As in: "I noticed something I'd like to share with you. Are you interested in hearing it?" Or simply, "Can I share some feedback with you?" Once they say "yes" (and who wouldn't?), it evens out the power dynamic, makes it easier for you to speak, and prepares the other person to accept the feedback more openly.

Second, *don't hedge.* When we are uncomfortable criticizing, we try to reduce the impact by reducing the criticism. Sometimes we sandwich the criticism between two compliments. But hedging dilutes and confuses the message. Instead, be clear, be concise, use a simple example, make it about the behavior, not the person, and don't be afraid of silence.

Third, *do it often.* That's how you create a culture in which people are open and honest for each other's benefit. If you only offer feedback once in a while, it feels out of character and more negative.

Of course, not all feedback needs to be critical. Positive feedback is excellent at reinforcing people's productive behavior, encouraging them to use their strengths more effectively and abundantly. Offer it frequently. Just do so at a different time than when you share the critical feedback.

"May I offer you a thought?" I asked James as we finished up our conversation.

"Please do," he responded.

"Not telling Ron that he drones on is hurting him, you, and the business. I know you feel bad sharing the criticism, but in this particular case, choosing not to share this feedback is a selfish behavior. You're hurting him in order to avoid your own discomfort. He needs—deserves—to know, don't you think?"

Silence. It was an awkward moment.

Which, it turns out, is a useful catalyst to action. James thought for a moment and then picked up his BlackBerry and e-mailed Ron, asking him to meet later that day.

> Although we often avoid giving critical feedback because we don't want to hurt the other person, the nicest and most helpful thing you can do for someone is to be honest and direct with them. Giving critical feedback with respect will help you build a deeper relationship with them.

• • • •

# 46 "Actually, There Is Something . . ."

## Accept the Gift of Criticism

"PETER, THERE'S SOMETHING WE WANT TO TALK TO YOU ABOUT," Mark said as we were sitting on the ground eating dinner. It was the summer of 1990, and Mark, Rich, and I were instructing a National Outdoor Leadership School (NOLS) course, leading about fifteen students for a month in the Wind River Mountain Range in Wyoming. Our students were at their own campsites nearby, preparing to sleep. I looked at Mark and then over at Rich. Both were staring at the ground.

"What'd I do?" I joked. Rich shifted uncomfortably as Mark continued.

"Actually, there is something . . ."

I felt my muscles tense and my adrenaline flow as they told me I was talking too much, spending too much time with the students. They thought I needed to separate myself more, be quieter. I asked them a few questions to understand their perspective better, but it was hard to really take in their answers as my mind raced:

*I thought the course had been going terrifically well. Do they want me to be just like them? But they're aloof and distant! That's just not my style! Anyway, are the students complaining? It should be a good thing that I'm spending time with our students! When was I talking too much? Are they right? Maybe I'm not made to be a NOLS instructor. Why are they ganging up on me?*

After that the course that summer went downhill for me. I became self-conscious and awkward, second-guessing every interaction I had with students and with my coleaders. On that trip, I let the perspective of my peers—valid though it may have been—emotionally overpower me.

But that was twenty years ago. Now I take criticism right in stride.

Yeah, right.

As a writer who publicly speaks about myself, I am vulnerable to criticism, which, at times, people deliver in personally biting ways. Once I wrote an article about finding a way to talk a manager into taking back a purchase beyond the two-week refund period, and I received a lot of strong criticism. People called my behavior unethical. Disingenuous. Manipulative. Materialistic. Deplorable.

*Wait,* I want to say, *you don't know me. I'm not any of those things.* But clearly, to many people, my article communicated that my actions were. And when I sat down to write my next piece I found myself hesitant, unsure of my writing, concerned about how it would be perceived.

Any criticism can be hard to accept. But surprise feedback—criticism that seems to come from nowhere, about an issue we haven't perceived ourselves—is the hardest. We're far more likely to be defensive.

The challenge of accepting criticism is not just about *admitting;* it's about *perceiving.* Before we can accept something, we have to become aware of it. Like the criticism I received on the

NOLS course, the feedback to my article completely blindsided me. I had no idea people would react the way they did, no sense that I was writing anything controversial. That kind of feedback exposes you to yourself, which is why it is both tremendously unsettling and exceptionally valuable. It's also why our defensiveness is so predictable and so counter-productive. The things we most need to hear are often the things we defend against hearing the most.

To take in surprise criticism more productively, we need a game plan. As you listen to the criticism and your adrenaline starts to flow, pause, take a deep breath, and do the following:

*Look beyond your feelings.* We call it constructive criticism, and it usually is. But it can also feel painful, destabilizing, and personal. Notice, and acknowledge—to yourself—your feelings of hurt, anger, embarrassment, insufficiency, and anything else that arises. Recognize the feelings—label them even—and then put them aside so the noise doesn't crowd out your hearing.

*Look beyond their delivery.* Feedback is hard to give, and the person offering criticism may not be skilled at doing it. Even if the feedback is delivered poorly, it doesn't mean it's not valuable and insightful. Not everything will be communicated in "I" statements, focused on behaviors, and shared with compassion. Avoid confusing the package with the message.

*Don't agree or disagree. Just collect the data.* If you let go of the need to respond, you'll reduce your defensiveness and give yourself space to really listen. Criticism is useful information about how someone else perceives you. Make sure you fully get it. That means asking questions to further explore what you're being told.

Probe. Solicit examples. You may even play devil's advocate, pushing the criticism back on itself, in the spirit of understanding it more fully. If you're worried that will look defensive, then explore the criticism with a third party instead. After receiving critical comments to my article, I asked several people—trusted friends who know me well enough to be honest with me—whether they saw what some others who were critical saw.

*Later, with some distance, decide what you want to do.* Data rarely forces action, it merely informs it. Recognizing that the decision, and power, to change is up to you will help you stay open. Once you've got some time, space, and grounding, think about what you heard—what the data is telling you—and make choices about if, what, and how you want to change.

Sometimes, you'll choose to change your behavior. I learned a lot from reading comments to my article and discussing them with others. I realized that what I considered playful, others saw as hurtful; that to experiment for my own gain is ethically questionable; that my message can be lost when my examples are controversial; and that I have to be careful about my tendency to put my needs over the needs of others.

But sometimes, you'll decide not to change your behavior and that perhaps you're better off staying the same and changing your surroundings. After that NOLS course, I led several more expeditions, but I never felt that I could live up to my colleagues' expectations of a quiet, authoritative, slightly removed outdoorsman.

Eventually, I left NOLS and joined the HayGroup, a consulting firm in the New York area. In my first week, I remember sitting quietly on a client call led by Andy Geller, a senior partner.

About twenty minutes into the call, he pressed the mute button and said, "Peter, say something. Anything. I know you can add value to this call, and the client needs to know it too."

He turned the sound back on, and I smiled, thinking, "Talk more? I like this consulting thing!"

> Next time you are blindsided by criticism, avoid reacting defensively. Criticism can be an incredible gift, if you are able to pause and look beyond your feelings and the delivery, collect good data, and decide, later, what to do with the feedback.

● ● ● ●

# 47  Crying About a Gift

## Create a Safe Space
## for Yourself and Others

"PLEASE, DADDY, PLEASE? CAN WE OPEN OUR PRESENTS FROM YOU now?"

It was the third night of Hanukkah, and Eleanor, our three young children, and I had just come home from a holiday party.

"Didn't you guys get enough presents at the party?" I asked. Dumb question.

"Okay," I relented. "Go ahead."

They ripped through the wrapping paper to expose their gifts. Little fairy-tale lanterns. As they began to play with their lanterns, one of my daughters began to notice some differences between her lantern and her sister's. She began to cry.

"My lantern door doesn't open. And it doesn't play music."

How ungrateful, I thought and took a deep breath to stave off my angry response. I immediately regretted letting her stay up so late, eat so much sugar at the party, and open that last gift. As she began to fall apart, I shifted from anger to reason. I told her that both gifts were nice and that she should feel happy about getting so many presents.

"I know, Daddy, I'm sorry. I usually love my gifts. But this time . . . I don't know. Why doesn't my door open?"

She wasn't angry, she was sad, and that softened me enough to hear Eleanor's voice in my head: *Just validate. Repeat back what you're hearing. Be a mirror.* I slid from reason to compassion.

"I'm sorry you feel so disappointed with the gift you got. You usually feel good about your gifts, but not this time. You're sad the door doesn't open like your sister's."

She kept crying. But to my utter amazement, what she was crying about abruptly changed.

"I was teaching everyone to make origami and everything was fine, but then Tammy started to teach them, and I grabbed the origami from Tammy. I don't know why I did it. I couldn't control it. I lost my temper, and then they didn't want me to teach them. They didn't want to play with me."

"Are you talking about the party, sweetie?"

"Yes," she said between sobs, "at the party. I don't know why I did it. And then they made a band but didn't want me to join, but I really wanted to."

Now I was crying with her. She wanted so badly to have friends, and she tried so hard but it was tough for her. That was why she cried when she received the present. It wasn't about the present. She'd been working hard all night to keep it together, and she just couldn't do it anymore.

I used to wonder why my daughter would often break down at home: What are we doing wrong? But what I've come to realize is that she might be breaking down because of something we're doing right.

The world can be a punishing place. It can feel unsafe to expose our feelings to others. Home—with Eleanor, with me—is a safe place for her to feel. To fall apart, take a deep breath, and rebuild. To have her feelings met with love, acceptance, and understanding.

This is a story about my home and my child, but it's also a story about your workplace and your employees, manager, colleagues, and clients.

Love, acceptance, and understanding in the workplace? Really? What's that got to do with performance?

Everything.

A group performs best when the people in the team know they can trust and depend on each other. Then they break out of silos. They take accountability for their own mistakes instead of blaming each other. They surface problems before they become major obstacles. But if people spend their energy hiding their feelings, that energy will leak out in negative and insidious ways, sabotaging your efforts and theirs.

If I'd stayed with reason instead of understanding, my daughter would have felt worse about herself. We never would have gotten to her sadness about the party, and I wouldn't have been able to help her with her real issue, namely, how she was getting along with her friends.

How do you do it? It's actually very easy. *Take a deep breath and just validate. Repeat back what you're hearing. Be a mirror.*

If it's easy, why don't we all do it all the time? Because there's a hard part too: managing your own discomfort. Can you be okay with the feelings of others? Can you listen without judging? Can you listen even though you might feel threatened?

As I was putting my daughter to bed, she asked me to lie down with her and talk, which we did for a while. She apologized for her response to the gift even though, she told me, she still wished her door opened.

"I know you do, sweetie. I'm sorry it doesn't open. And I'm also sorry you had a hard time at the party."

She turned over to face the wall and shut her eyes. There was a moment of silence as she was beginning to drift off to sleep. Then she reached behind her and took my hand, hugging it to her chest.

"I love you, Dad."

"I love you too."

And, as we both feel asleep, her final gift of the night— acceptance—had become my gift too.

> Our tendency to hide our feelings often back-fires as those feelings seep into our work in negative ways, sabotaging our efforts. Create a safe environment for you and others so you can perform at your best.

● ● ● ●

# 48 I Don't Miss a Thing

## Stop Checking E-mail

RECENTLY, I TOOK A WEEKLONG TECHNOLOGY-FREE VACATION WITH my family: no computer, no phone, no e-mail.

After the trip, when I returned to the office and checked my computer, I had hundreds of e-mails waiting for me. I took a deep breath and started in on them. Three hours later, my inbox—a week's worth of messages—was empty.

Contrast that with my experience the next day, and each day after that, when I spent well more than three hours each *day* on e-mail. Some of that time involved back-and-forth e-mailing, but still, the difference is dramatic.

I've come to the conclusion that I use e-mail to distract myself. Whenever I feel the least bit uneasy, I check my e-mail. Stuck while writing an article? Bored on a phone call? Standing in an elevator, frustrated in a meeting, anxious about an interaction? Might as well check e-mail. It's an ever-present, easy-access way to avoid my feelings of discomfort.

What makes e-mail so compelling is that it's so compelling. I wonder what's waiting for me in my inbox? It's scintillating. It also feels legitimate, even responsible. I'm *working*. I need to make sure I don't miss an important message or fail to respond in a timely fashion.

But it's become a serious problem. When we don't control our e-mail habit, it controls us. Everyone I know complains about e-mail overload. E-mail pours in, with no break to its flow. And like addicts, we check it incessantly, drawing ourselves away from meetings, conversations, personal time, or whatever is right in front of us.

It's not just the abundance of e-mail that's our problem—it's the inefficiency in how we deal with it. Each time we check our e-mail on the fly, we lose time pulling out our phones, loading the e-mail, reading new e-mails without taking action on them, and rereading those to which we haven't yet responded. Then, back at our computers, we reread them again.

The inefficient way we deal with e-mail is rattling us. According to *USA Today,* the number of lawsuits filed by employees claiming unfair overtime is up 32 percent since 2008. The major reason for the increase? E-mail on devices like smartphones is intruding on our personal time.[12]

The solution, I believe, is hidden in my postvacation e-mail experience. Instead of checking e-mail continuously and from multiple devices, schedule specific e-mail time during the day while you are at your computer. All other time is e-mail vacation time.

We are most efficient when we answer e-mail in bulk at our computers. We move faster, can access files when we need them, and link more quickly and easily to other programs like our calendars. Also, when we sit down for the express purpose of doing e-mails, we have our e-mail heads on. We are more focused, more driven, wasting no time in transition from one activity to another.

I bulk process my e-mail three times a day in thirty-minute increments, once in the morning, once mid-day, and once before shutting down my computer for the day. I use a timer and when it beeps, I close my e-mail program. Outside my designated e-mail times, I don't access my e-mail—from any device—until my next scheduled e-mail session. I no longer use my phone for e-mail unless I'm away from my computer all day.

E-mail is the perfect application of what I call "action-inaction." When you're on e-mail, be on e-mail fully; do nothing else. When you're off e-mail, be off e-mail completely. When the urge to check arises—and it arises often—I take a deep breath and feel whatever feelings come up. And then I focus on whatever I'm doing, even if what I'm doing is waiting. I let my mind relax.

Here's what I've found: I don't miss a thing.

In fact, it's the opposite. I gain presence throughout my day. I am focused on what's around me in the moment, without distraction. I listen more attentively, notice people's subtle reactions I would otherwise overlook, and come up with more ideas as my mind wanders. I'm more productive, more sensitive, more creative, and happier.

I'm also going through my e-mail faster and with more attention than before. I don't make those I'm-moving-too-fast mistakes like copying the wrong person or sending an e-mail before finishing it or saying something hurtful. So I'm also more efficient.

But what if someone needs an immediate response? Worrying about that is precisely the kind of misguided rationalization that reinforces our addiction. I haven't angered anyone with my new process. In fact, I don't think anyone has noticed my mini e-mail vacations because responding to an e-mail within a few hours is perfectly reasonable. And, in the off chance that they need a response within minutes, they'll find another way to reach me, either by texting or calling.

E-mail is no longer an overwhelming burden to me. I'm spending an hour and a half a day on it, which for me is the right amount. You may need more or less time per day. Experiment and then schedule the appropriate time slots.

The hardest part is resisting the temptation to check during your off–e-mail hours. My advice? When you have the urge to check your e-mail, check yourself instead. What's going on for you? What are you feeling? Take a deep breath, and relax into an undistracted moment.

For a brief moment in the middle of a hectic workday, it just might feel like you're on vacation.

> To improve your productivity, check e-mail only a few times a day. When you feel the urge to check your inbox, take a breath and check yourself instead.

• • • •

# 49 The No-PowerPoint Rule

## Embrace the Informal Meeting

"THAT WAS DREADFUL. NOT ONLY WAS I BORED; EVERYONE ELSE was bored too. Disengaged. I'm terrible at facilitating these kinds of meetings. But they're so important. I've got to get better at it. I need to find a better way."

I wrote that in a journal entry about seven years ago. I still remember the meeting that finally drove me to change how I run meetings. There were about ten people involved—the CEO and his direct reports—and we met for two days off-site in a hotel so we wouldn't be distracted. The goal was to discuss and agree on a strategy for the next year.

I had prepared meticulously. I met one-on-one with each person on the team and collected their thoughts about the strategy of the company and what might get in the way of its successful execution. Using their input, I designed the flow of the two days and asked each person to prepare a PowerPoint presentation of the strategy for their area.

The result? When each person stood up to present his strategy, everyone else did one of two things: tune out or poke holes.

Most presentations elicit those reactions because most presentations are polished and thorough and designed to satisfy their audience, as well as to build confidence that the speaker knows what he's talking about. People tune out because nothing is required of them. Or they poke holes because if they don't tune out, it's the most interesting thing to do when someone is trying to prove there are no holes.

So over the following seven years, I experimented with meetings. I did team-building activities; I stayed at the front of the room throughout the meeting; I took myself out of the meeting completely; I taught skills critical to the meeting like communication and team dynamics; I had the CEO run the meeting; I took the CEO out of the meeting completely; and dozens of other tweaks.

Over time, I identified a single factor that makes the biggest difference between a great meeting and a poor one: PowerPoint. The best meetings don't go near it.

PowerPoint presentations inevitably end up as monologues. They focus on answers, and everyone faces the screen. But your meetings should be conversations. They should focus on questions, not answers, and people should face each other. I know it sounds crazy, but I've found that even the hum of the projector discourages dialogue.

Meetings are exorbitantly expensive when you add up the number of highly paid people in the room at the same time. You should use them as a time to engage deeply in issues, not to update each other on progress.

Try this. Instead of preparing clear, well-thought-out (and boring) PowerPoint presentations, try leading informal discussions, using flip charts to collect important points, draw conclusions, and agree on action plans with owners and timelines.

Save some time at the end of the meeting to develop communications plans to disseminate the decisions. I'm always a little surprised at how many inconsistencies and disagreements surface only when it comes time to commit to precisely what is going to be communicated.

There is, of course, a lot more that goes into a successful meeting. But following the no-PowerPoint rule has the greatest impact because it keeps the energy where it should be: solving problems together.

I always get a little nervous when I run a meeting because if it's run well, it's unpredictable. Ideas, insights, and solutions arise that never would have come up without the collaboration of the people in the room. Arguments can break out at any time. But what makes a meeting unpredictable is also what makes it exciting and valuable.

Last week, I spent two days running a strategy off-site with the CEO and leadership team of a large technology company that is experiencing the good, but very real, problems that accompany rapid growth. Each executive led a conversation, and each conversation ended with an agreed-upon action plan with owners and timelines. All this was accomplished without the background hum of a projector.

At the end of the meeting, after a two-hour conversation about communicating our decisions to the rest of the organization, the CFO—a true cynic when it comes to spending (wasting?) time in meetings—turned to me with sincerity and said, "That was a really useful way to spend a couple of days."

Coming from him? That's journal-worthy.

It's all too easy to default to preparing overly thought-out (and boring) PowerPoint presentations. Instead, try leading informal discussions. People collaborate best when they think together about problems that cross their silos.

• • • •

# 50 The Pea Haters Who Ate Peas Like Pea Lovers

## Tell Stories to Get Others to Change

**"I'D LIKE TO TALK TO YOU ABOUT A BIG PROJECT," THE WOMAN TOLD** me on the phone.

She was a senior leader in a professional services firm, where people really are their most important asset. Only it turns out the people weren't so happy. Theirs was a very successful firm with high revenues, great clients, and hard-working employees. But employee satisfaction was abysmally low, and turnover rates were staggeringly high. Employees were performing; they just weren't staying.

This firm had developed a reputation for being a terrible place to work. When I met with the head of the firm, he illustrated the problem with a personal example. Just recently, he told me, a client meeting had been scheduled on the day one of his employees was getting married. "I told her she needed to be there. That the meeting was early enough and she could still get to her wedding on time."

He paused and then continued, "I'm not proud of that story, but it's how we've always operated the firm." Then he looked at me, "So, Peter, how do you change other people?"

I've often heard people say that you can't change other people; you can only change yourself. But, the reality for many of us is that we're constantly trying to get other people to change. Parents try to change their children's behavior, spouses and partners try to change the behavior of their significant others, and people at work are trying to change each other's behavior all the time.

Still, most of the time, we fail, or worse, we encourage the exact behavior we're trying to change. Our failures aren't for lack of trying, and they're not because the task is impossible. It's just that the way we try to get people to change is often counterproductive.

So what do we usually do that doesn't work? We try to tell people what to do, often in anger or frustration. Or we try to reward people, financially or otherwise. We send e-mails and communications to highlight what we're looking for. And we try to punish people who don't follow our direction. None of that seems to work predictably.

So, if none of those things work, what does?

In the late 1970s, University of Illinois researcher Leann Lipps Birch conducted a series of experiments on children to see what would get them to eat vegetables they disliked.[13] This is a high bar. We're not talking about simply eating more vegetables. We're talking about eating specific vegetables: the ones they didn't like.

You could tell the children you expect them to eat their vegetables—and reward them with ice cream if they did. You could explain all the reasons why eating their vegetables is good for them. And you could eat your own vegetables as a good role model. Those things might help. But Birch found one thing that worked predictably. She put a child who didn't like peas at a table with several other children who did. Within a meal or two, the pea hater was eating peas like the pea lovers.

Peer pressure.

"Stories." I said to the head of the firm.

"Excuse me?" he responded.

"You change other people with stories. Right now your stories are about how hard you work people. Like the woman you forced to work on her wedding day. You may not be proud of it, but it's the story you tell. That story conveys what you expect of people simply and reliably. And I'm certain you're not the only one who tells it. You can be sure the bride tells it. And all her friends. If you want to change people's behavior, you have to change the stories they hear and the ones they tell."

I told him not to change anything else—not the performance review systems or the reward systems or the way people are trained. Don't change anything. Not yet anyway. For now, just change the stories. For a while there will be a disconnect between the new stories and the old ones. And that disconnect will create tension. That tension represents the transition from the old behavior to the new one. If you stick with it, over time, the new stories will take hold.

To stimulate people's change all you need to do is two simple things:

1. Do dramatic story-worthy things that represent the change you want people to make. Then let other people tell stories about it.

2. Find other people who do story-worthy things that represent the change you want people to make. Then tell stories about them.

For example, if you want people on your team to move faster and focus less on perfectionism, move quickly on an issue by sending out an e-mail with typos in it. Or if you want people to communicate more effectively, stop checking your computer in the middle of a conversation every time the new message sound beeps; instead, put your computer to sleep when they walk into your office. Or if you're trying to increase people's happiness at work, instead of making the bride work on her wedding day, give her the week off.

We live by stories. We tell them, repeat them, listen to them carefully, and act in accordance with them.

We can change our stories and be changed by them.

> Often, the way we try to get people to change doesn't work and ends up encouraging the exact behavior we're trying to change. Since we tend to conform to the behavior of the people around us—and that behavior tends to conform to the stories people tell and hear—create change by telling the right stories.

● ● ● ●

# 51  How Jori Lost Eighty Pounds

## Forget Willpower. Restructure Your Environment.

"I WANT TO RUN SOMETHING BY YOU," I SAID TO MY FRIEND JORI WHO has lost eighty pounds over the past six months. "Our ability to lose weight is based on our willingness to suffer through discomfort, to be a little hungry, and yet to resist the temptation of eating."

"You're wrong," he said. "You don't know what my hunger is like. It's painful. Withstanding it might work for a week or two, but not for the long term."

I immediately knew that Jori was right. Discipline, willpower, and self-control are unsustainable. Eventually, we weaken. I've tried to lose weight in many different ways. Only two have worked: (1) I cut refined sugar out of my life. I threw out all the ice cream, candy, cookies, and cake and restocked my shelves with healthier alternatives; (2) I signed up for a meal-delivery service. Each morning, for a month, they delivered all my carefully portioned meals and snacks for the day. The food was delicious and satisfying, and I only ate what they gave me, nothing more.

In both situations I reduced my need for discipline. I changed the environment around me so that it was more likely that I would make the choices that were in my best long-term interests.

"So, how did you lose your weight?" I asked him.

Jori had Lap-Band surgery, which physically constricted the top of his stomach. As Jori eats, his upper stomach fills up, trickling food to the rest of his stomach, making him feel full sooner and for a longer period of time.

In other words, Jori didn't lose weight by withstanding the discomfort of hunger. He lost weight by eradicating the discomfort of hunger. Jori's surgery created a situation that made his desired behavior—eating less—not just more likely, but inevitable.

"When will you take off the Lap-Band?" I asked him.

"Never," he told me.

The Lap-Band can be tightened to create a smaller opening to the stomach or loosened to allow people to eat with less constriction. Some patients choose to loosen their Lap-Bands when they want to enjoy unrestricted eating, like during vacations or holidays.

You would think that after years of eating smaller portions with a tightened Lap-Band, people would have developed new eating habits they could sustain when the band is loosened. But that's not the case. According to Jori's doctor, people easily gain twenty pounds or more in a month.

In other words, it's great to learn new habits, but if we want to sustain them, we need to change our environment, and then maintain that new environment, for as long as we want to maintain our change. If you want to keep the weight off, don't put sugar back in your cabinets, or loosen your Lap Band, or consider food outside your agreed-upon portions.

One of my clients, Lisa, was having difficulty with one of her direct reports, David, who wasn't communicating clearly or frequently enough. We created a list of questions that Lisa and David went through each day to help him communicate better. Questions like "Is there any one you need to update today? Anyone you need to thank? Anyone to whom you need to ask a question?"

After three weeks of answering those questions daily, his communication improved greatly, so Lisa stopped asking the questions. Within a few days, David fell back into his old uncommunicative patterns. The questions didn't fix David; they merely shaped his behavior while he was using them.

So the question is, Have you structured your environment—your life—so that you are more likely to accomplish your most important priorities?

For many of us, the answer is no. We start a day with great intentions. But then people start calling and e-mailing, asking and directing, and soon we can hardly remember what we wanted to focus on in the first place—if we ever knew. Our days begin to look like frenzied, attempts to get traction while making little headway. By the end of a week, we've forgotten what it was we were hoping to accomplish at the beginning of the week. And by the end the year, we're frustrated that we haven't moved forward in our most important priorities.

The solution isn't willing yourself to focus better. That won't work. Discipline and self-control are unsustainable because in most of our environments, there are too many distractions, too many things other people want us to do, too many opportunities and temptations that draw us away from lives that reflect our true values and priorities. It's like trying to lose weight while living in a candy store.

We need to restructure our environments—like constricting our stomachs or emptying our cabinets—so we are more likely to move forward on our most important priorities.

Here are three ways you can restructure your environment:

### 1. Empty your cabinets of sugar.

Identify up to five things—no more—that you want to focus on for the year. Those are where you should spend 95 percent of your time. Take anything that doesn't fit into one of those areas of annual focus, and get it off your to-do list. I've created a to-do list that's made of six boxes—one for each of my five areas of focus and the sixth labeled "the other 5 percent" That other 5 percent box is like sugar—a little might be okay, but your day should never contain more than 5 percent of the activities that don't fit into your five areas of annual focus.

### 2. Constrict your stomach.

Each morning, take a look at your six-box to-do list and transfer the most important items to accomplish for the day into time slots in your calendar. That way, you'll make strategic choices about fitting the most important items into the limited space of your day.

### 3. Make a firm agreement with someone about what you're going to eat.

Sit down with someone else—your manager, a colleague, your partner—and show them your six-box to-do list and your calendar for the day. Tell them what you plan to accomplish and how it fits in with your plan for what you want to focus on for the year. Saying it out loud and having another person hear you and reflect back what they hear creates a deeper level of commitment and accountability.

Because, like Jori's success losing weight, your success focusing on the things that matter most to you, will only happen—in the long term—when you create the environment that supports it.

> Relying on willpower is an uphill, never-ending battle. Instead, structure your environment and life so that you are more likely to accomplish your most important priorities.

• • • •

# CONCLUSION

**"YOU'RE VEGAN? AGAIN?" NICKY LAUGHED. "DIDN'T YOU ALREADY** try that?"

"Why don't you just eat normally—everything in moderation?" Pam chimed in.

Everyone at the table laughed, partly at me, partly at Pam, who, well into her second mojito, was hardly the poster child for moderation. I was with my high school friends; the six of us have been meeting for dinner once a month for over twenty-five years. We don't stand on ceremony.

The conversation didn't last long; no topic ever does at these dinners. But it did get me thinking. Am I a failure because I'm vegan again? Why couldn't I sustain it last time? And if I couldn't, why am I trying again?

One way to look at it is that behavior change is like quitting smoking or alcohol; sometimes it takes several tries to permanently follow through on a commitment. But there's another perspective that's also true: not everything needs to be sustainable. It all depends on what you want to achieve.

I was leading a strategy off-site with the CEO and leadership team of a technology organization whose revenues exceeded $600 million. We'd spent several days redesigning parts of the organization: we created a new organizational structure, put people in new leadership roles, and clarified accountabilities. This was an excellent company with capable leadership, a solid strategy for growth, and credible targets to become a billion-dollar company within a few years.

Referring to the new organizational structure we had collectively designed, one of the CEO's direct reports spoke up. "This won't work," he said "At $900 million it will be unwieldy."

The CEO reflected for a moment and then replied, "It doesn't have to work at $900 million. It has to work for now. We'll change it again, probably at $750 million."

Brilliant. Mostly, things are useful for a particular time. Then they're not. For many things, it's better to have a temporary solution that you're willing to change than a solution you think is permanent and that, as a result, you get stuck on.

Process re-engineering? The one-minute manager? Management by objective? Guerrilla marketing? It's easy to dismiss them all, and so many other ideas, as fads. Here one day, gone the next. Better not to get sucked into them in the first place. But instead, consider how each "fad" might have been useful, perhaps in your organization, for a period of time. And that might be just fine. For something to be a great success, it doesn't have to last forever.

The challenge? Not thinking of any solution as a cure-all in the first place.

When we think of something as a panacea, we ignore its weaknesses and negative side effects, and eventually, when the inevitable flaws are exposed, we lose faith in the solution completely. We discount any value it provided. Because it never lived up to our expectations, it never *fully* worked. And then we go off in search of the next magic bullet.

Our yearning for *the* solution, the formula that will solve all our problems, the panacea to our angst, is strong. It's also misguided because nothing is perfect, and nothing lasts forever. So we're better off seeing every solution as temporary and every tool as potentially valuable and probably fleeting. That's true whether the change is personal (like a new diet) or organizational (like a new management tool, a new organizational structure, or a new diversity program).

Seeing every solution as temporary yields surprising dividends:

- It becomes easier to commit to. If we know it's not perfect and not forever, why not give it a whirl?

- It becomes easier (and faster) to implement. If we know the initiative isn't forever, let's not make it perfect; let's just make it work.

- It becomes easier to get others involved. If we acknowledge that a solution is imperfect and unfinished, other people are more likely to participate in improving it, which gives them a sense of ownership.

- It becomes easier to pay for. If we're not going to make it perfect, and it's not going to last forever, let's not invest a huge amount of capital up front.

- It becomes easier to let go when appropriate. If we haven't invested a huge amount of money, or our identities, in the solution, we'll waste far less time and energy evangelizing about how great it is and holding tight even when it no longer adds value. Certainty, when it contradicts the evidence, is never a good thing.

These five side effects of an it's-not-forever mindset drastically increase the chance that you're going to do something instead of just think, talk, plan, and argue about doing something.

We change. Situations change. The people around us change. And the tools we use should change too.

A few guidelines:

- Distinguish between a commitment to an outcome—like marriage, staying sober, being healthy, having a profitable organization—and a commitment to the tools you use to fulfill or achieve that outcome. The tools can be fleeting while the outcome can be permanent.

- Understand the value you're getting and why. Then decide on the evidence that will indicate it's no longer providing that value. That way you'll know when it's time to move on.

- Decide when you're going to reassess. It doesn't help to constantly second guess yourself. That makes it impossible to follow through; you'll give up in a moment of weakness only to regret it later. Instead, decide when you're going to reassess, and commit fully until then.

*Four Seconds* is filled with ideas, strategies, and tactics that can help you make smarter decisions—and take more impactful actions—in the moment. Some of these approaches will be just right for you now. Others may be more helpful later. Allow yourself the flexibility to put into practice what works for you and keep using it as long as it's working. When it feels less effective, peruse *Four Seconds* again and see what resonates. Just remember to take that deep breath, pause, and make a deliberate choice that will get you where you want to go.

When I decided to cut meat and dairy out of my diet, I was feeling overstuffed. I wanted to feel clean again, and going vegan helps me do that. Also, what I know about myself is that, when I'm feeling overwhelmed and out of control, I do things that help me feel back in control—like cut my hair or cut things out of my diet. It's a coping mechanism that helps me feel less overwhelmed in the rest of my life. When I'm feeling back in control, I'll probably change my diet again.

It's also good to remember that just because you don't have to commit forever, doesn't mean everything will be short lived. "Some things, like my dietary choices, are fleeting," I told my old classmates toward the end of our dinner, "Live with it. You don't have to make the same choices, and I'll probably be eating differently next time we meet."

"But don't worry," I added. "Other things, like our dinner tradition, will go on forever."

# ACKNOWLEDGMENTS

WHEN YOU'RE ALONE, TAPPING AWAY ON A KEYBOARD, STARING AT A screen, watching the words appear one letter at a time, slowly forming sentences, paragraphs, pages, and eventually, chapters, it's easy to fall prey to the illusion that you are the sole creator of your work.

But that is hardly the case.

There are so many people—by their influence, their support, their actual work—without whom this book would not be in your hands at this moment.

Yes, I wrote this book. But Genoveva Llosa and her team at HarperOne did a marvelous job of refining it, playing with its parts, and editing it. Thank you, Genoveva, for your belief in me, your enthusiasm about this book, your vision of what it could be, and your tireless drive to make it stronger. You're a pleasure to work with, and I love how you shaped it. And great thinking on the title, Hannah.

And while writing a book is one challenge, selling it is another. Jim Levine and his team at the Levine Greenberg Rostan Literary Agency did that and much, much more. Thank you, Jim, for being so thoughtful, so supportive, so committed to me and to my writing. You are a fabulous partner—smart, steady, present, and caring. It is a joy to work with you.

Every piece of writing goes through many revisions and edits, and there are a number of people who refine my work before it's ever seen in public. A huge thank you to Katherine Bell, my editor at *Harvard Business Review,* who has been editing—and shaping—my writing for many years. You are a fantastic editor, Katherine, and I am so grateful for your continued support of my ideas and my voice.

This book represents the culmination of years of writing. And my years of writing represent the culmination of years of experiences and lessons from some very special people who remind me, every day, of what it means to be supported, loved, challenged, and taught.

Emily Cohen, you have more than a great eye for writing; you are a clear North Star for me and a great reminder of what's important to focus on and what's okay to let go of. Thanks Em, for your belief in me and your willingness to throw all of what you have and all of who you are into our work together. I am so thankful for you and so grateful that we're in this together. I picked the right one.

Jessica Gelson, thank you for the kind of love and support that I hope you feel back and that helps me believe in myself every day. I can't quite express to you how important our friendship is to me, but I know you feel it. The way you live your life, and the courage you show in your commitments to people and spirit, are a powerful model for me. You have a huge heart. Thanks, Jess, for being so solid and so loving.

Also, Jess, thank you for finally, after much prodding, introducing me to Ann Bradney. Ann, you have really changed my life. I listen, speak, write, even walk differently as a result of my work with you. I have learned of the importance of emotional courage from you, and I continue to learn so much from your example and from your teaching. Thank you, Ann, for working so tirelessly to help create a world I want to live in.

I am also deeply impacted by the people with whom I work, some for short periods (a weekend workshop at Kripalu or someone I meet at a speech I give), some for longer periods (every single one of you who have attended the Bregman Leadership Intensive), and some for years (my retained clients and colleagues with whom I work). Each interaction impacts me deeply; I take none of them for granted, and I am so grateful for those of you who trust me enough to delve more deeply into my work. Thank you.

And thank you to every one of you who reads my blog and my books, who takes the time to e-mail me or post a review; I don't take those things lightly, and I so appreciate knowing that what I write, what I do, matters. It's what gives me the energy to keep doing it.

Finally, and definitely not leastly, I am so, so filled with gratitude for my family. My parents to whom I have dedicated this book, have taught me so much. Thank you, Mama and Papa, for having such strong belief and faith in me. Your confidence gives me the courage to take the kinds of risks that excite me, make me happy, and make me proud. I owe so much of it to you.

Isabelle, Sophia, and Daniel, I learn from you every day. Isabelle, I am touched by how deeply you feel and how authentically you live your life. Your thoughtfulness, sincerity, sensitivity, and courage is awe inspiring. I strive to be as real as you. Sophia, you are such a joy to be around. Your giggling brings me so much happiness, and I am tremendously moved by your kindness. You always look at the good side of people and situations; your generosity of spirit is a model for me. Daniel, your wild and enthusiastic engagement with the world gives me energy. Just watching you—in pillow fights, launching off the dock, even reading a book—makes me smile. And your curiosity and drive to understand the world around you helps me understand things more deeply too. The three of you live life so fully. I am grateful for every part of who you are, even as that changes with your growth and experience. I feel so privileged to be entrusted with your care, and I am so grateful for every moment I get playing, reading, swimming, skiing, biking, eating, and just being with you.

And Eleanor, my love, anything I write on these pages will not be enough. I am beyond grateful for our relationship, for the way you trust me enough to share your deepest self, for your trustworthiness that allows me to share mine, and most importantly, for the care and love with which you hold my soul.

# NOTES

1. The research is based in the famous marshmallow experiment conducted on four-year-old children in the 1960s by Walter Mischel, a professor of psychology at Stanford University: www.ocf.berkeley.edu/~rascl/assets/pdfs/Berman%20et%20al.,%20Nature%20Communications%202013.pdf. See also I. M. Eigsti, et al., "Predicting cognitive control from preschool to late adolescence and young adulthood," *Psychological Science* 17 (2006): 478–84; W. Mischel, et al., " 'Willpower' over the life span: decomposing self-regulation." *Social Cognitive and Affective Neuroscience* 6 (2011): 252–56; W. Mischel, Y. Shoda, and M. L. Rodriguez, "Delay of gratification in children," *Science* 244 (1989): 933–38; and Y. Shoda, W. Mischel, and P. K. Peake, "Predicting adolescent cognitive and selfregulatory competences from preschool delay of gratification—identifying diagnostic conditions," *Developmental Psychology* 26 (1990): 978–86.

2. Lisa D. Ordóñez, Maurice E. Schweitzer, Adam D. Galinsky, and Max H. Bazerman, "Goals Gone Wild: The Systematic Side Effects of Over-Prescribing Goal Setting" (working paper, Harvard Business School Working Knowledge, February 11, 2009), http://hbswk.hbs.edu/item/6114.html.

3. Alisa Tugend, "Experts' Advice to the Goal-Oriented: Don't Overdo It," *New York Times,* October 5, 2012, www.nytimes.com/2012/10/06/your-money/the-perils-of-setting-goals.html?_r=0.

4. Lesley Alderman, "Money Tips for When the Sniffles Start," *New York Times,* January 1, 2010, www.nytimes.com/2010/01/02/health/02patient.html.

5. Rossana Weitekamp and Barbara Pruitt, "Number of New Companies Created Annually Remains Remarkably Constant Across Time, According to Kauffman Foundation Study," Kauffman Foundation, January 12, 2010, www.archive-org.com/page/298632/2012–09–13/ and www.marketwired.com/press-release/Number-New-Companies-Created-Annually-Remains-Remarkably-Constant-Across-Time-1184493.htm.

6. "Louis CK interview 2000," interview by Conan O'Brien, *Late Night with Conan O'Brien,* NBC, November 28, 2000, video posted on lalarikyu's YouTube channel, April 10, 2009, www.youtube.com/watch?v=gRIfvJhTk_Y.

7. Fast Company Staff, "The 100 Most Creative People in Business 2011," *Fast Company,* May 18, 2011, www.fastcompany.com/3018427/most-creative-people–2011/21-chris-cox.

8. W. Dunn, L. B. Aknin, and M. I. Norton, "Spending Money on Others Promotes Happiness," *Science* 319 (2008): 1687–88.

9. Del Jones, "Best Friends Good for Business," *USA Today,* December 1, 2004, 1B. http://usatoday30.usatoday.com/educate/college/careers/hottopic31.htm.

10. "Close High-School Friendships Point to Higher Wages," *The Daily Stat* (blog), *Harvard Business Review,* June 25, 2010, http://web.hbr.org/email/archive/dailystat.php?date=062510.

11. Don Steinberg, "The State of Our Football Is Strong 44 Presidents. XLIV Games. One Strange Idea." *The Philadelphia Inquirer,* February 5, 2010, http://articles.philly.com/2010-02-05/news/25218548_1_presidents-super-bowl-xxvi-barack-obama.

12. Paul Davidson, "More American Workers Sue Employers for Overtime Pay," *USA Today,* April 19, 2012, http://usatoday30.usatoday.com/money/jobcenter/workplace/story/2012–04–15/workers-sue-unpaid-overtime/54301774/1.

13. Leann Lipps Birch, "Effects of Peer Models' Food Choices and Eating Behaviors on Preschooler's Food Preferences," *Child Development* 51 (1980): 489–96.

# INDEX

# ABOUT THE AUTHOR

**PETER BREGMAN** is the CEO of Bregman Partners, a firm that advises, coaches, and trains leaders at all levels to take powerful and ambitious actions to achieve the things that are most important to them and their organizations. He runs leadership programs and consults with and coaches leaders, helping them build strong organizations of people who work courageously together to drive stellar results. He wrote *Point B: A Short Guide to Leading a Big Change* and the *Wall Street Journal* bestseller *18 Minutes: Find Your Focus, Master Distraction, and Get the Right Things Done,* which was winner of the gold medal from the Axiom Business Book Awards, named the best business book of the year on NPR, and selected by *Publisher's Weekly* and the *New York Post* as a top ten business book. Featured on PBS, ABC, and CNN, Peter is a regular contributor to *Harvard Business Review, Fast Company, Forbes,* NPR, *Psychology Today,* and CNN. He lives in New York City with his wife and three children. He can be reached at www.peterbregman.com.

To download helpful *Four Seconds* resources, go to www.peter bregman.com/four-seconds.